....

WAKEFIELD METROPOLITAN DISTRICT LIBRARIES

This book must be returned by the last date entered above.

An extension of loan may be arranged on request if the book is not in demand.

Readers should make the fullest use of the library service asking for any books and information they need.

Headquarters: Balne Lane   Telephone 371231/4
              Wakefield

Goon with the Wind

Goon with the Wind

Max Geldray

with John R. Vance

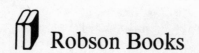 Robson Books

First published in Great Britain in 1989 by Robson Books Ltd,
Bolsover House, 5-6 Clipstone Street, London W1P 7EB

British Library Cataloguing in Publication Data

Geldray, Max
 Goon with the wind: an autobiography of Max Geldray.
 1. Jazz. Harmonica playing. Geldray, Max
 I. Title
 788'.9

ISBN 0 86051 578 8

Typesetting by Picador Graphics, Bristol
Printed in Great Britain by St. Edmundsbury Press Limited,
Bury St. Edmunds, Suffolk.

Contents

Introduction   9

1 My Family Beginnings   11

2 Mac Geldray and his Mouth Accordeon Band   23

3 Sprouting out from Brussels   36

4 Personalities in Paris   48

5 Fleeing to Freedom   59

6 Soldiers in Exile   80

7 Battlegrounds   96

8 The Coming of the Goons   109

9 Peter Sellers   126

10 Changes   156

11 The Last Goon Show of All   165

12 The Final Phase   171

To my wife Susan and to our children Judy, Holly, Timothy and Philip and in memory of my parents and my little sister Xaviere.

I have been greatly encouraged by a number of people while writing this book. In particular I would like to thank: Michael Bentine, Susan Geldray, Ron Moody, Jeremy Robson, Dr Roger Blomquest, Harry Secombe, Philip Geldray and also Angela Morley, who started the ball rolling by interviewing me about my life story on tape.

Introduction

THIS IS NOT a book full of celebrity gossip, and anecdotes about who did what to whom. I hope I can tell you a story which is much more than that. Certainly there is much to tell about the Goons. About jazz. And about the early, early days in music. But fundamentally this is a book about a lifetime — about me and the people I knew.

March 1985 may seem an odd place to start it but in that month there was a day which re-opened a great many things in my life. And really caused this book to happen.

I was at home in Palm Springs, California. It was mid-afternoon on a stunningly sunshiny day. If you have a picture in your mind of palm trees, oasis vegetation, warm breezes and the sight of snow-capped mountains from a desert floor, then you have the right picture.

Michael Bentine had just left my house. He is a winter neighbour of mine and a great friend. He was, of course, one of the original Goons, appearing on the very first show that Harry Secombe, Spike Milligan and Peter Sellers worked on together, even before the series was known as the Goon Show. So our friendship goes back all the way to the early days of 1950. Michael is a writer, among a great many other things, and he had brought over one of his books for me to read.

A number of times over the previous few years he had suggested to me that I should write a book. My answer had always been that I was not a writer, that the things we talked about happened a long time ago and that people wouldn't be interested. What was more important to me was the voluntary work I did — and still do — at the Betty Ford Center, where people go for treatment of their problems with alcohol and other drugs. I played the harmonica occasionally, I intended to rest on my oars.

Of course that was the wrong thing to say to the astonishingly

9

versatile Mr Bentine — comedian, raconteur, lecturer, and writer of novels, essays, scripts and articles: a man who can also talk learnedly and convincingly, at a mile a minute, on all manner of subjects. But he'd surprised me that time.

Michael had looked at me thoughtfully for several quiet moments. Then he had said, 'Max, you don't have to stop at just *resting* on your oars. You can put them right away. Lie back. Don't move. But let me tell you, old friend, I think you have an interesting story to tell! And you are not old bones yet. Why don't you row a little bit longer?'

I still wasn't convinced, yet his suggestion did stay in my mind. Partly because, earlier, some other people had mentioned it too. I don't want you to think that people were breaking down the door to get the Max Geldray Story, but the subject *had* come up on several occasions and from unexpected sources, too.

After Michael had left I was in the house alone with my dog, Mickey. Mickey is a tiny little creature, with curly white fur and the face of an angel. But in spite of the angel face, he's a feisty little critter with the heart of a piranha who especially likes ankles. Just then, he started to bark. He wanted to get out to attack the postman's leg. I waited until this potential victim had left and then went out to the mailbox to collect my bills, junk mail and magazines. It turned out there was something else too. A large brown envelope from Holland.

I tore it open on the way back to the house and several heavy pieces of metal fell to the ground. When I picked them up I discovered they were medals — four military medals — decorations for serving in the Princess Irene Brigade in the Second World War!

Now admittedly the Dutch government was a wee bit tardy delivering these decorations, since the war had been over for forty years! But I was overwhelmed with all kinds of feelings and pictures and memories of events suddenly fresher in my mind than things that had happened to me just a month ago.

Those medals made me feel very proud. And they started the sequence of events that led to this book, for I really did start to think about people and other times and other places. And I began to write down some of my memories. Now I will begin at the beginning.

1

My Family Beginnings

I WAS BORN in Holland — Amsterdam to be more precise — in the year 1916, the first-born of Leon and Margarite van Gelder. There is a province in the eastern part of Holland called Gelderland, and I would like to think that it was named after my forebears. But it is quite possible that my forebears arrived from somewhere in the East, with one of those names about seventeen syllables long, and simply 'Dutchifyed' it when they settled. When you translate 'van Gelder' into English, it means 'from Gelder', so it is more than likely we picked up our name that way.

In my mother's case I do know that the surname Biallosterky was changed to Biallo. I remember once hearing her joke that the family had changed their name because of her, Biallosterky being far too long a name for a girl who was only four foot ten!

My father's family had been in Holland a very long time, and they seemed to have spread all over the country and worked in almost every possible trade — although I don't recall that any of them was terribly successful.

My mother's clan was quite the opposite. They were a very prosperous lot, in the diamond business. They were to be found in cities such as Amsterdam, Brussels and Antwerp. My mother could be said to have grown up with the proverbial silver spoon.

We were a Jewish family. I suppose we maintained our Jewishness in a tribal sense; but, as far as I can recall, religion was not really a factor in our lives.

I cannot remember any religious observance in our house, or even among our relatives. We kept no Sabbaths, and had

11

none of the religious artefacts to be found in Dutch Jewish homes. But my parents did lead very principled lives in terms of their values and the way they treated other people. Theirs were good standards to be influenced by.

The most vivid memories I have of my mother are from the days just before I reached my teens. The photos from our family albums don't reveal it, but she had been a wisp of a girl — someone they might have referred to in those days as 'small-boned'. I am not particularly tall (five feet seven and a half inches in my prime), but by the time I was twelve, I could stand beside her, look down, and feel tall. Her hair was very dark, and even in the middle of summer her skin stayed alabaster white. Even though she had a full, round face, there was always something of the waif about her. I am sure it had to do with the small, shy smile she had almost continuously at the corner of her mouth.

My father gave me his looks: black, wavy hair, a slightly crooked grin and the dark, sharp features we have come to think of as swarthy and Mediterranean. My father was a travelling salesman, covering much of western Europe, and so he was away from home for long stretches of time. It is one of the reasons that I have few clear memories of him from my childhood.

But there are other reasons why I know so little about the lives of my father and mother. And these are less easy to understand. It is true to say that the Dutch, as popularly believed, are a very conservative people, and this conservatism includes the way Dutch families display their affection for each other. The van Gelders were not a family which hugged and kissed, and their emotional reactions were always very discreet. Indeed, after my sister and I had grown out of babyhood, our parents were seldom outwardly affectionate to us. Or to each other, for that matter. It wasn't that they were uncaring: often I could feel their affection when I looked into their faces, but it was an affection which they would almost never display openly.

And just as affection was kept inside, so were family confidences. For this reason, I have no details of my parent's young lives: how they met; where they were married; how long they were married before I was born; or even an accurate way of knowing how old they were when they were killed. And I know very, very little about their hopes and aspirations. By the time I was old enough, and perhaps sensitive enough, to consider asking these questions, there was no one left to ask.

What I do know is the day-to-day life we led, and the social scenes which, I suppose, moulded my values and the patterns of my life in so many subtle ways.

After that description of my parents, it would be easy to think of them, and the Dutch generally, as joyless people. They were far from that. I think the memories that are most vivid in my mind are of the times when we had parties at our house.

Both my mother and father loved to have people come to the house: relatives, friends, acquaintances, and even people they had scarcely met. And so our house was filled each Saturday night, and for much of Sunday.

The party would begin in a very formal way, with the men in the parlour sipping their Genever (that most potent of Dutch gins) while the ladies sat in another room. And, to say the very least, the ladies were most decorous in their behaviour. In fact they did not even drink. Well, not exactly.

The Dutch middle class appeared to believe that it was unseemly for females, married or single, to imbibe. This might lead you to believe that the Dutch ladies were a sober, and a sobersides, contingent. But there was a loophole.

The women were allowed to partake of Advocaat. If you have never had Advocaat served to you, and had it served in the Dutch way, I will describe it to you. Advocaat is an extremely thick yellow substance made of a combination of brandy, sugar and eggs. When it was first introduced it was somehow adopted as a drink for lawyers — hence a name which has its root in the word 'advocate'. Somewhere along the way it lost favour with lawyers, but at the same time gained immense favour as a social beverage for the ladies. You will notice I did not call it a drink!

Ladies partook of Advocaat by pouring it into a special glass. The glass was about four or five inches tall, and was very narrow; the opening at the top was about the size of an old shilling or an American fifty-cent piece. When the liqueur was put inside, it was so thick that the women had to drink it with a long-handled teaspoon — which obviously took it out of the class of an alcoholic drink.

Even though the women sipped it a spoonful at a time, they still seemed to be able to put the stuff away at a fairly rapid pace. Since it was potent (probably just as potent as the men's Genever gin) the mood would soon change. The women would then feel free to join the men in the parlour. My father would sit down at the piano, and the singing would begin.

I have always thought of Advocaat as the social alchemy of Dutch life. It also produced a number of children. But there were other things which affected our lives as a family, and some of them were much more serious than Advocaat. If I were to make a list of what had a profound effect, that list would certainly include wars. Three of them, to be exact. Sometimes those effects were oblique, but they still turned out to be profound.

From about 1912, my father had become one of the few prosperous van Gelders. He had taken all his savings and become a working investor for a famous Spanish perfume-maker. It was a good business move, because the company had created the famous perfume known as Maja. But by the time I was born, in 1916, the First World War was changing all that.

Although Holland was neutral, the markets for perfume were not. My father's business was reduced to a trickle, and he found himself striving to avoid bankruptcy. Throughout those years the three of us lived in a cramped and dingy little flat in Amsterdam, very near to poverty. My mother had never known hardship before, and she was profoundly influenced by it. By this time I was two years old, there had been a war for my entire life. But at two years old you are hardly affected by a war across a border, and you aren't aware that your family's standard of living has plummeted. And then the war ended, and as quickly the pendulum swung dramatically the other way.

It is hard to understand how, with all the post-war devastation, and with millions of people in Europe rebuilding their lives, the perfume business could suddenly begin to prosper! But it did. And by 1920 my father was the European manager for the company, and making an astonishingly good living.

Some time in 1922, when the family fortune had grown large enough, my father decided that we should have a house in the country. I was six years old when he found the house of my mother's dreams. It was about twenty miles from Amsterdam, in a very conservative and orderly little community called Bilthoven.

I know that when you are young the world looks larger and different; and that's an illusion that sometimes shocks you later on in your life. I've had that experience of going back to a place years later, and having the feeling that the place had shrunk and lost the elegance I'd remembered. But I wasn't fooled about that house in Bilthoven. It was palatial.

At that time, many houses in Europe were given names by the people who owned them, and my father did exactly that with ours. Above a front window, carved in a style that looked like Cyrillic script, were the words Casa Myrurgia. Father had decided to name our house after the town in Spain where the wondrous Maja was manufactured. No doubt a tribute to our good fortune.

The house sat on two acres of land. It was two and a half storeys high, with great square rooms, and in the entrance hall a grand staircase, endlessly long and winding and elegant, with a marvellous banister for sliding down. Can you imagine what it was like to move from a cramped flat in Amsterdam and then find ourselves there?

There is always a price to pay for space and elegance, and to keep Casa Myrurgia in Dutch good order was no small task. When I mention 'Dutch good order' I should explain that the Dutch have a fervent wish to be clean. Perhaps even 'fervent' isn't a strong enough word! You know that old saying 'You could eat off the floor'? Well, 'Dutch clean' means you can drink soup through a straw out of the crevices.

We had a maid to do the housework, a weekly cleaning lady for the heavy cleaning, and a laundress. Every week my mother and the housemaid would take all the bedding and then all the mattresses outside for airing. Next they would take all the furniture from downstairs and put it outside for airing, too. Then, to complete the job, they would take down the drapes and curtains from the wall. The place was so bare that the cleaning lady could have washed it down with a fire-hose!

But I believe there was another reason why my mother went to all this length, beyond sharing the national obsession for 'Dutch clean'. Casa Myrurgia was the pride of her life. It was a symbol to her that the past was over!

There was always music in our home. My father was one of those 'play by ear' pianists — the type who could play the newest pop song after hearing it once on the radio. My mother, if you will pardon a bad pun, was at the other end of the scale. She was classically trained, and her repertoire was more along the lines of Mozart and Brahms. I once overheard an aunt and uncle talk about the fact that she had been a child prodigy in Holland, but by the time I knew her she was simply someone who played the piano for herself or her little son. I would sit on her lap and ask her to play nursery rhymes, while I imitated her by pressing my thumbs on any key that was available. It is why, even now, music always reminds me of warmth and family.

Since my mother was the one with the formal musical training, you might suppose that it would be she who would insist that I had some musical education. Instead it was my father. I was sitting there one night, ardently trying to make some pleasant sounds on our upright, when my father decided he cared for something a little more melodic.

The teacher they hired was a very proper, sober and matronly lady, with the big, lank frame of a Dutch farmer's wife. There was a darkish line of hair above her lip, like a young boy's moustache. And she had shoulders, wrists and rough hands that looked as though she had spent more time churning cheeses than playing the piano.

I know it is very unfair to this lady, but I think I saw my music teacher as some arch villainess from a boy's annual. To begin with, I couldn't believe she loved music. Secondly, I saw her as someone who would dole out the punishment if I didn't deliver. So, as intimidated as I was, I think the moment we began the lessons my mind was programmed not to learn.

Three times a week she came to teach me the piano and assign long practices. I don't believe I ever practised one of the pieces — but I did fool her for quite a while!

Just at the end of our lesson I would ask her to play my homework-piece for one more time. Then, lo and behold, the next time she arrived I would be confident, and sounding as though I had actually put in some practice time.

The simple truth is that I was a sneaky devil. In all the time we spent together I had never learned to read the notes. I had simply memorized the sound. It was a blessing that I had inherited my father's talent — I could hear something a few times, and then simply recite it back. But it was unfortunate that I didn't seem to have a brain in my head when it came to interpreting music that was printed on paper.

One day she asked me to play something, and then handed me the wrong piece of music. Being handed the wrong thing would not have been serious — if I had noticed! But I was so busy pretending to concentrate on the notes that I wasn't aware that the sheet of music didn't have the right title. The irony is that I remember I played the wrong tune quite well. Still, it didn't seem to satisfy her!

Out of the corner of my eye I could see her face at my side, and I was bewildered when I noticed that it had begun to tighten. A line of scarlet splotch seemed to be moving down from her hairline. I stopped playing! She didn't say a word, but spluttered out a deep-throated sound, and turned a darker shade of crimson. I moved my hands quickly from the keys, certain she was about to slam the lid on my fingers.

Moments later, I could hear my teacher talking to my mother and father in the kitchen. She was defaming me in one of those grating voices — the sound equivalent of being poked in the eye with a sharp stick. I am very grateful that my mother and father did not heed her suggestions for punishment. It is very unpleasant to be maimed for life in the way she suggested!

After about half an hour the piano teacher was gone, and so were my lessons. After a short while of scolding and pleading, my parents seemed to resign themselves to the fact that I had a musical blind spot. But it was really more than a blind spot. I think it was a very clear illustration of how my brain works when it comes to music. Will it make sense if I say that, to this day, I can see the music inside my head? I know, it sounds odd to me too! I certainly can hear the music in my mind very acutely — but I can't imagine reading notes.

In 1928, when I was twelve, there was a dramatic change in the musical part of my life. In spite of the fiasco with the piano lessons, from the time I had been a toddler I had been crazy about music. But there is a difference between loving the sound of music around you, and being serious about it as part of your life. It was only when I found the 'right' music that it really became a part of my life.

A friend of my father's gave him a huge radio. It was a magnificent receiver, with a dial that was crowded with short-wave and long-wave bands. Suddenly, I was hearing broadcasts from France, Germany, England, Luxembourg, Belgium, and from short-wave stations all over the world, including programmes of music I had never heard before. I was hearing jazz — American jazz — Louis Armstrong jazz.

At that time jazz was in its infancy, and probably something of an acquired taste to most of those who claimed to like it. But how could anyone *not* love its energy, its vitality and the freedom of its form? And Louis Armstrong, among all the players, became something special to me. Over the years there have been times when I have tried to explain Satchmo Armstrong's specialness, but any real understanding has to come through feelings. Trying to explain it in words is like trying to explain how a great operatic aria can make you cry. I can only find one comment that I can make easily about Louis Armstrong's music. His trumpet was more than simply a horn — it had all the expression and the passion of a human voice.

To give you an idea of the extent of my love for jazz, I have to talk for a moment about my radio studio. I had a very large bedroom in Casa Myrurgia with a very large cupboard for clothes. I decided that this was a terrible waste of space, and that if I dumped my clothing in drawers and piles underneath the bed, the closet could become a perfect (if airless) radio studio. My mother took some convincing, and insisted on several changes in my plan, but finally agreed. I used to go in there and play the part of a radio announcer, announcing titles over a small, tinny-sounding microphone. Then I would let loose the sound of Louis. Of course the only place the sound went was to a small radio speaker in another room, but there I was: Holland's first jazz disc jockey. I got very, very hot in there. But I didn't quit for that reason. It was because I was afraid that my records would warp!

Until 1927 we were a family of three, and then my sister Xaviere was born. I was eleven, and it was more than a little difficult to share my life, and my parents, with a new baby. I loved her, and paid attention to her, but the gap in our ages meant that she was less like a sister and more like some new element in my life.

The most vivid recollections I have of her are of her sickness and her singing. She had asthma, which seemed to restrict her in everything she tried to do. And yet she looked so healthy, with rosy cheeks, rich, dark, curly hair and short chubby fingers. She was a child who loved to smile — and she loved music too! I thought that was wonderful, although there were times when I acted as if I didn't.

Whenever I passed by little Xaviere there was a very strong chance that she would be either singing or humming. It should have made me smile to hear her tiny voice; but sometimes, being a teenage boy, I had great and important things to concentrate on. Then it seemed incessant! I remember that often I would scold her, and order her to stop because it was bothering me. She would obediently stop. Then, because she was only a child, she would forget my scolding and begin to sing again.

By the time she was eight I was off pursuing my life as a musician. She was to be killed before she reached her fourteenth birthday.

Today, when I look through my album of pictures and see my parents and my sister — my father looking formal and unsmiling, my mother, a serious-minded matron, and Xaviere a small, dark, sad-eyed girl — the pictures don't correspond to my memories. I remember them as fun-loving and very warm people, and these black and white images seem so sombre. One of the big regrets in my life is that we spent so little time together. Though I didn't realize it, Xaviere had been born just as the family fortune went into decline again, and we all seemed to have too little time for each other.

I was fifteen in February 1931. I would be dishonest and ungrateful if I didn't describe my life at that time as idyllic. I went to a nice school and lived in a big house. I was part of a family which had money to travel, and a taste for the better things of life. But there had been subtle changes in the world around us, and over the next six months these became downright ominous.

The first thing I noticed was that my parents seemed to stop buying so many things. Then they tightened up on the help for the house. They entertained far less often. They never mentioned it, but now it was obvious, even to me, that my father's business was in trouble.

Part of it may have been the result of the 1929 Stock Market crash. A great many people were now managing without luxury products; a few were even jumping out of windows. But there was another reason for the decline of my father's business. For the second time in my brief lifetime the shadows of war were looming — this time in Spain.

Maja, the perfume on which we depended, was manufactured in Spain, and in April 1931 King Alfonso XIII was deposed and Spain was declared a republic. The republic decided that the profits of a bourgeois perfume business should belong to the state, especially since the principal owner of Maja was known to have been a Royalist. Our fortunes came crashing down. Casa Myrurgia was gone, and so were almost all the things that had been in it. We moved back to Amsterdam, into the same district we had lived in before. I have a vivid memory of the first time I entered that small flat. Although we had lost so much, it seemed cluttered. I went into the kitchen and found my mother sitting on a chair, holding her head in both her hands. It was the same day they sold the piano. Both my mother and my father were silent for days after that.

My mother lost her youthfulness overnight. There was a serious grimness about her jaw, and in her eyes. Life at home did not seem to have much fun and laughter in it, and so I began to spend more and more time away from home. Like a thousand thousand sons and daughters before me, I didn't pause to understand the cause. I left, and felt a burden lifted from my heart.

My mother never recovered from this second loss. It wasn't the loss of our home and the luxury that made her change, it was the loss of hope. My father's business was in a shambles, and he seemed changed and shrunken into someone eaten by his failure. As though she was bearing the strain too, my sister became continuously ill with chronic asthma. And although it wasn't life-threatening, it was life-curtailing. In me, my mother saw encouragement. And when I found my chance to move away, it turned out that she was the one to spur me on.

Although it was a time when many boys of my age went out to work in permanent jobs, my father insisted that I continue at school. It was a great financial hardship for them, so I wish I could say that I was a successful scholar. But school was never a profitable experience for me. I always felt that I was marking time, waiting for something else to happen. Then, on my sixteenth birthday, my father decided that I should get some training in the world of business, and he arranged with a friend to hire me. I started off as a stock-boy in the fabric section of a large department store. I didn't hate it. But I didn't exactly like being up to my neck in wools and cottons and silks and satins either! Music wasn't just a dream to me. It was a promise of escape.

2

Mac Geldray and his Mouth Accordeon Band

AT CERTAIN TIMES of the year, one of the most noticeable things about the climate of Holland is that there is a tendency toward dampness and rain. But, because sea-level Holland has very sandy soil, there is a rapid run-off of this excess water. This is fortunate, because otherwise the Dutch would have to travel by boat, and enter their houses through second-storey windows. As it is, fungus grows directly out of their wooden shoes!

It was in such a season (though it was not actually raining at the time), in February 1930, that I rode my bicycle in the heart of Amsterdam. I was on my way to the Tuchinsky Theatre — actually a cinema, but one that had been built with a big stage.

The Tuchinsky was similar to many theatres which flourished when vaudeville was at its peak. It wasn't very much to look at from the outside: there were no flashing lights, just a couple of thin romanesque columns, and a few steps up to the double doors at the front. But once inside it looked enormous to me. There was a wide marble staircase, and chandeliers filled with hundreds of lights. Even if I stood at the back of the balcony the stage still seemed large, with its immense, curved proscenium arch and the heavy velvet curtain. Outside that, there was a large area for the orchestra, then seats that went on and on into the darkness.

The man who owned the theatre loved the business, and somehow it seemed he couldn't see himself abandoning vaudeville. The Tuchinsky Theatre showed feature films,

23

but between these showings the stage would be lit up, and the pit band would strike up the overture for the vaudeville acts, some of which were fairly big-time. I used to dream of being part of all that. I would save my money and go inside, sit as close as I could to the pit, and stay there in the dark until I was thrown out. Often I sat through the same picture several times just to see the stage show again.

But much of the time I didn't have any money, so I would just stand in the alleyway that led to the stage door. There was a large window to ventilate the projection room, and it stayed open while the stage show was on. I could stand there and listen.

On this February afternoon, as I stood in the alleyway, it started to rain — softly at first, but soon pelting down from the roofs of the buildings on either side of the alleyway. And, no matter how closely I hugged the wall, the water ran like high tide down the back of my collar, filling up my shoes. They weren't wooden, but I could almost feel the fungus growing. Then a wind came up. Between the downpour and the howl of the wind, I couldn't hear a single sound, so I decided to go down the street and seek refuge in a music shop.

The shop was owned by a man named Hans Mossel. It was small, but it was stuffed full of instruments.

The reason Mossel's Music stocked everything you could blow, tap, bang, pluck or strum, was that Mossel's life was music! And Mossel loved jazz! For this reason it was acceptable for a semi-penniless, eighteen-year-old jazz buff to drop in. Or should I say drip in?

There weren't any customers inside, so Hans had been sitting there with the lights out, looking at the pelting rain and the afternoon sky the colour of pewter. He pulled down a blind on the front door proclaiming the store was closed, handed me a cloth to wipe my wet face, and went off into the back of the store to make some hot tea.

The light in the room was growing darker and darker, but we sat there for a very long time in the comfort of that cosiness, sipping tea and talking about music.

It began with quite an innocuous remark. I mentioned that

I had been listening to the BBC and had heard a man playing a mouth organ. But that it sounded quite different from anything I had heard before.

'Ah, yes,' said Hans, 'it's a harmonica! It has all the notes and half-notes. You see, Max, all the mouth organs you've heard before were diatonic. They could only play a limited range of whole notes. It is why you could only play simple tunes on a mouth organ — why it's a child's instrument! This new one is different. It's a mouth organ with a slide — a chromatic slide.'

It turned out that Hans knew so much about this subject because he had recently received from the Hohner company in Germany a pamphlet about their new instrument, the harmonica. Hans had ordered one. He offered to let me buy it. It would be there in a week.

I suppose it is some strange quirk of my memory that makes me unable to remember much about learning to play that harmonica. Of course there was no one to teach me, because the instrument literally had no players. But I do remember that, for the next while, there seemed to be nothing else in my life. And sometimes, when I was practising in our cramped little flat, my father would say to me, 'Max, could you do something else? Collect stamps? Anything!'

My mother was much more indulgent about the sounds I was making. 'You're getting better, Max,' she would say. 'But you really should take some time to eat!'

It was a Saturday, about two months later. I was on my way to the Tuchinsky Theatre to see a 'talking' film. Since I was going by the door I thought I would drop in and see my friend in his music shop.

Hans asked me, 'How's the harmonica going, Max?' So I pulled it out of my pocket and started to play. Hans listened for a while, then he went over to the door, pulled down the 'closed' blind, and we spent the entire afternoon playing our own musical interlude in the store.

I missed seeing my very first talking picture that day, but I cannot tell you about the pride of being praised by this

professional musician. It set me on the road to being one,
too. Throughout the years that followed I met Hans Mossel
on several occasions. He kept his music shop, but he had
also formed a dance band for one of the first radio stations
in Holland. The band was called the Daisy Bells. It pleases
me to tell you that he was very successful, and his Daisy
Bells became very famous on Dutch radio.

Every time I met Hans after that he would say to me,
'How's the harmonica going, Max?' And then we would
laugh at our running joke. I am very grateful to Hans Mossel
— and for the way it rains in Holland!

By 1934 I had been playing the harmonica for about two
years. My career was moving at a snail's pace — a very sick
snail at that. I had made a few appearances on Dutch radio,
but nothing seemed to come of them.

In those days the Dutch were in some respects a strange
breed. Holland is a country which is small in size, and has
a population of some twenty-odd million. Being
surrounded, as it is, by people who speak other languages
and have other cultures, one might expect the country to
protect its identity by being a little insular. But, at the same
time, since it lies on the border of those most confident of
cultures, the French and the German, and since its people
speak English, French and German as a matter of course,
and since its own culture is rich in art and music and history,
one might suppose that this 'cosmopolitan effect' would
induce a strong sense of self and considerable
self-assurance. This is far from the case. Even as the
Dutchman brags about himself, one feels it is less in the
sense of 'Look at me. I'm better!' and much more 'Look at
me. I'm not so bad!'

Twice during my appearances on Dutch national radio I
was asked to change my name. Van Gelder I was told, was
too Dutch. So much for Dutch insularity, nationalism, and
being a prophet in your own land. I remember thinking the
upside-down and foggy thought, 'How will I get well
known if I change my name?'

I didn't change my name, but I did begin to realize that if

I was going to have a career, it would probably happen outside my own country.

I had reached the ripe old age of seventeen, and I had all the feelings of mid-life crisis. Here I was getting on, and nothing seemed to be happening to me. My first step wasn't to leave the country, but to do a little redirection. I had listened to Borah Minovitch and his harmonica band on the radio, and even seen one of their appearances in a film. They were now known internationally. And even if it was true that they were more a novelty act than a musical act, almost single-handedly they had made the harmonica a part of the music world. I decided that a harmonica group was the thing of the future.

Because there weren't many good harmonica players around, recruiting people was a frustrating job.

At last I found eight other boys, all around my own age, and with great enthusiasm we set off to practice ourselves silly. Building a repertoire was even harder!

Some of the other boys were musically well educated, but I found that I was the only one who could do any arranging. Since I didn't read music, I had to do it all in my head. I would think the music through, and then play each part and rehearse each player. It took a long time, but it seemed to work.

As anyone who has ever played in a modern rock band will tell you, the most important decision of your professional life is what you name the group. Since I could play rings around everyone else, and was doing nine-tenths of the work, the boys insisted we call ourselves 'The Max van Gelder Harmonica Band'. I didn't put up much resistance to the idea, but the name didn't last very long.

One afternoon, with about two carloads of confidence, all nine of us set off to find ourselves a theatrical talent agent. To this day I am stunned at the fact that we found anyone who would take this rag-tag group of learners seriously. The agent turned out to be a very short and stocky man, a Mr Franklyn, who seemed to be extremely excited about our prospects and suggested that — if we would put up just a

few guilders — he could make arrangements for our
first-ever publicity stills.

I cannot tell you how excited we were when we first saw
those stills, although a little bemused by the fact that we had
been renamed. The part that said 'E. Franklyn presents'
belonged of course to our agent. The harmonica had been
simplified to the mouth organ — or rather, to something
termed a 'Mouth Accordeon'. And Max van Gelder was
renamed, too, because we were now billed as 'E. Franklyn
presents Mac Geldray and his Mouth Accordeon Band'.

I gave in on the name at the time, and the stage name
Geldray was to remain with me the rest of my life. But, later
on, I did make a small adjustment and reverted to Max. I
just couldn't get used to being called 'Mac'. With my
accent, who'd have believed it — even if I'd worn a kilt?

For a long time after that we still didn't get any work or
offers. And then one day our agent sent a message — and
then we met the acrobat.

The acrobat was an American: a big burly guy who had the
rough, square-jawed look of a Marlborough cowboy, tall,
strong and hairy. I don't remember his name, but I do know
he billed himself as 'the King Kong of Acrobats and Strong
Men'; the film had recently caused a stir in Europe and, as I
was to learn, Mr King Kong was a man who believed in
trends. A year earlier he had swept into Amsterdam and swept
a girl off her feet. Now he had come back to see his mother-
in-law, who happened also to be an agent.

King Kong had been touring Europe for some time with
his own small band of players: a juggler, a comedian and
himself. Although he had been doing reasonably well, he
was looking to round out his programme. At the time I
wasn't too sure what King Kong meant by 'round out'. But
it did seem that our musical act was the rounding out his
mother-in-law had in mind.

The Mac Geldray Mouth Accordeon Band thought it had
struck professional gold, because King Kong turned out to
be thrilled, enthralled and sold. He pranced around showing
off his biceps to the short, stocky Dutch kids, telling us he
was going to give us our first break. We were going to appear

in his show on a stage in Belgium! I am grateful to him for
the thought. However, as well as being the first break, it also
turned out to be a bad one.

The scene was the capital city of Belgium, Brussels. The time
was eight in the evening. We were appearing in a large hall,
and the programme seemed to start on exactly the right note.
Though people were spread out, and seated a distance from
the performers, the audience was large and appeared to be
both warm and enthusiastic. The comedian made them laugh.
The juggler dropped only one pin. And King Kong contorted
himself into odd shapes and made wondrous flips in the air
— proving he was either very double-jointed, or that he had
just broken all the major bones in his body. All the omens
seemed right!

But then it was our turn. King Kong's instincts in
recognizing a musical novelty act might have been bang on,
but his idea of how to use one was bang off. At our first
meeting, he had insisted that our group play his original
compositions, and that he would act as the on-stage
conductor. The terrible truth is, that while King Kong may
have been able to bend his spine in half — and lift objects
I couldn't even drag — his musical compositions wouldn't
have made the Hit Parade's top ten thousand.

If the music was bad, trying to hear it was worse. This
cavernous hall was frequently used for cattle shows — and
had the perfect acoustics for bovine attractions. It was in
this atmosphere that the nine of us were supposed to crowd
around a single microphone and create subtle and exciting
harmonies. This in the early 1930s, when most microphones
were used glued to your lips — because they had all the bass
response of a nail on a blackboard. Our hoped-for success
was a long shot.

At first the audience was very patient about hearing
snatches of what appeared to be music. Then it seemed they
were yearning to have the cows back, because they seemed
to be mooing! Soon we discovered it wasn't moos, it was
boos!

Humiliated, we walked off the stage. 'Never mind,' said

King Kong but his face was the colour of beetroot. Later, he handed us an envelope with some money in it. But he didn't come to the station to bid us goodbye.

I learned two lessons from that experience. One was about sound, and the other was about being prepared to meet an audience. Some of the other members of the Mac Geldray Mouth Accordeon Band learned something too; half of them quit the harmonica business and went back to life's serious work.

The four of us who were left — Hank, Gert, Rob and myself — were, as it turned out, the best players. And now we began to work in earnest. If we weren't world-beaters as a musical act, at least we were a manageable size. Our agent had dropped us but, miraculously, it wasn't very long before we had our second show-business nibble.

Though I have often had arguments with agents (generally minor, and most often about very little bits of money), they have always played a large role in my life. Not in the way of managing my career, but by opening unexpected doors for me. First, King Kong, the acrobat, had been married to the agent's daughter; on the next occasion it was I who was taking out an agent's daughter. Such is the fickleness of youth that, while I can remember she was pretty and quiet, I can't remember what she looked like, or even her name. But I do remember that one day she took me home to play for her father.

He was a very short, wiry man with hawk-like features and, unlike his daughter, he was not quiet! He moved about the room with fast, sharp movements. He moved continuously, waving his hands, swinging his arms, turning his head, as though he was trying to deal with the news that his family had just been beheaded, or was having an epileptic seizure! When I had finished, I had not the slightest idea of what he thought about the playing. Suddenly, without a word, he dashed to the telephone.

It turned out that the person on the other end of the phone was a very popular English comic, by the name of Tom Moss.

Moss had come to the Continent looking for novelty acts for his vaudeville company, and he was spending a few days in Amsterdam. When he heard about me he must have expressed interest, for the next thing I knew they were telling me, in Dutch, that this big time show-business person was coming straight over to see me. By the time Tom Moss arrived at the house I had gathered together the other three players of our group.

If someone eats a lemon in front of a harmonica player, or makes him extremely nervous, the player will sometimes pucker up and salivate, and end up making those sounds that approximate a high-pitched gargle. On the other hand, sometimes the nervous tension can make the mouth tight and dry, so that the player ends up sounding as though the thing is being blown with the exhale end of a vacuum cleaner. Of the four assembled harmonica players, some were lemon-puckered, and some were tight and dry!

Fortunately, Moss smiled and listened attentively all the way through our mini-concert, and as time went on we got better. After the tenth number, he put his hands up, palms out, and said 'OK! OK!' We were hired on the spot.

We would be going on a tour of English theatres with Tom Moss. He was taking us on a six-week booking, and was going to pay us what sounded to me like an incredible sum of money. And he had already renamed our act. From then on we were to be called 'The Hollander Boys'.

Going back to the time long before Shakespeare, it is recorded that English theatre audiences were very much a part of the action. Beyond just hollering, applauding, hissing and booing the players, the audience felt it was their right to lose themselves in the event, as though it was a real happening. Sometimes plays were written so that the players could banter with the audience. Sometimes, villains had to be protected.

In some respects that spirit continued into the 1930s, when music hall vaudeville was at its height. People felt a part of this sort of theatre. There was a special warmth for old-chestnut skits, old jokes and favourite performers. And there were special in jokes, that people in another theatre in another town would never understand. There were sing-alongs and banter, and the audience would laugh, poke each other in the ribs, and stand and applaud their part of the show. It was a part of English social life, and I never saw anything like it in any other part of the world. Even from the stage, you could feel that you had to be a 'regular' to be *really* on the inside, and know what was going on.

The Tom Moss Theatrical Touring Company was part of that tradition, and a favourite in towns and cities all across the British Isles. It was a fair-sized troupe, made up of between twenty-five and thirty regular members, with Moss as the master of ceremonies and comedian. He and all the rest of the cast were pure music hall, and when they got on the stage they were cheered and hooted at like old friends.

Just before the chorus line and finale at the end of the show, the Hollander Boys appeared. I wouldn't call what we did an act, it was more a routine of musical numbers, interspersed with ear-to-ear nervous smiles.

At the best of times it was hard for a foreigner to understand what was going on in an English music hall. The fact that none of us understood English made it harder. The fact that we had a grand total of one night of stage experience complicated it further. It produced a bladder condition in a couple of us.

But, blessedly, Tom was a very shrewd showman, and so he built our image on those very same things. He told the audience that we were fresh from the tulip patch, had our first non-wooden shoes, had never been more than a bicycle ride from some unpronounceable place in Holland, and that we had no idea of what was going on! No doubt we were made the butt of some of the humour, but the British love an underdog, and we could tell that the audience, right from the very first performances, was on our side. So, if our staging and our playing wasn't quite up to snuff, they forgave us.

Often, when you don't know what you are doing, you find it is the time when you learn the most. I discovered a great deal about sound and about stagecraft during that time. I began to take longer solos with the group, and to take the microphone off the stand and cradle it against the harmonica. I was excited at the harmonica sound I was getting, and the intimacy I could feel in the music.

After the first week Tom Moss's troupe began to move around the country into the bigger towns, with theatres that were large and plush and clean. Our nervous excitement at being in England exhausted us. To four Dutch boys, who had their heart in music, England was a special place. This was the country which had originated most of the big bands we'd heard as youngsters on gramophone records and on the radio. (It is strange to think of it now, but in Casa Myrurgia I had even sat in the wonderful acoustic of the bath, and sung the songs of some crooner — imitating the words and emotions, and hardly understanding a word of the meaning.) And now here I was in England! I think, more than anything, I wanted to be English. And with the way my adrenalin was flowing, I was simply gobbling up the sound of the English tongue.

At first I was inseparable from the other Hollander Boys, but once I had acquired the basics of English I decided that speaking Dutch was getting in my way. And it was when I got to know one of the chorus girls that my language learning really took off.

Her name was Hazel, and I imagine she was all of nineteen or twenty. But she was English and she was a knockout, so she seemed very worldly-wise to me. Of course she wasn't, she was innocent and very simple. However alongside her I still felt like a Dutch country bumpkin.

In the evening, when Hazel and I left our theatrical digs to walk through the town, she would spend all her time teaching me English words and phrases, and squeezing my hand in encouragement.

As you can tell, it wasn't much of a romance, but it was profoundly comforting. Both Hazel and I found ourselves away, for the first time, from all the family, friends and places we had known all our lives. We travelled to strange cities and lived in very un-homelike boarding houses. And while I was learning something about being on my own, she was there, helping me get over the hurdles of being self-sufficient. Since those days I have had a special soft spot in my heart for English girls.

While I was learning about self-sufficiency, I was also learning about self-confidence. Confidence rubs off, and I could feel my confidence growing all the time. Part of it was simply from performing on the stage so regularly, but it also came from working with great professionals, like Tom Moss. He not only encouraged me, but he was responsible for my playing with a big-time orchestra for the very first time in my life.

I remember we had arrived in Liverpool and were opening at a theatre the next day. That evening Tom invited me and several other members of the group, to go along with him to a local dance garden where the Jack Hylton Orchestra was appearing. As we went in, Hylton himself waved at Tom from the bandstand. Tom turned to me and said, 'You'll meet him!'

I should explain that I had collected Jack Hylton recordings since I was a very young boy, and at that time the Jack Hylton Orchestra was certainly one of the most popular bands in all Europe. So when Tom Moss said that I was going to meet the great Jack Hylton, he immediately jumped from being someone I admired, to the level of legend.

During the first few hours that a club like this was open, the crowd came to dance. After an intermission, the dancing would stop and the star attraction would take over the stage. Well, it was intermission time, and Jack Hylton strolled over to our table. He was an elegant man, who stood very erect in front of the band. The way he waved the baton, in a great fluid motion, was more as if he were directing a symphony orchestra than a band playing popular hits of the day. After we were introduced I hardly said a word to him. I was then very surprised when Tom suggested that perhaps I might play a number with the band. There was a short silence. Then Hylton looked at Moss and grinned. Such was his trust in him that he simply said 'All right', and without another word began to walk back to the bandstand — motioning to me over his shoulder.

Apart from the couple of occasions when I had played on Dutch radio, I had never been a soloist or played with a dance orchestra before, but it seemed very natural to me. At the beginning only the piano player accompanied me, but then the other players started to weave themselves into the music — and it was full and lush and wonderful.

That was my first taste of musical heaven. And it planted a feeling in me about orchestras — a feeling that has never gone away. It also started the first stirrings of the thought that maybe I should not be part of a harmonica group. Later I had felt guilty about those stirrings, because I knew that somehow I was being disloyal to the other Hollander Boys: Hank and Gert and Rob.

3

Sprouting out from Brussels

THOUGH I WAS only away from Holland for nine weeks, I felt as if I had been away for months and months. The tour of England with Tom Moss had changed me and, from the moment I was back in Amsterdam, I felt out of place. I felt as though I had outgrown my home.

When I say 'outgrown', it sounds like conceit: as though I'm saying the country was too small for somebody as big-time as me. But it had to do with being where the markets were, and it had to do with being where I was accepted. In England, being Dutch had never mattered. But in Holland, with its very narrow entertainment business, being a native son seemed to make me something less than special. And the thought of having to settle for working in a department store was more than I could stand!

But there was another reason why I felt it was time to leave, and this was much more personal. I felt detached. Since we'd left Bilthoven, things had not been the same. Living where we did, and how we did, had changed my parents. Their mood, their hopes, and their interest in things around them, was quite different. I could look at them and see them fading — losing the brightness I had always seen in them. And although they both loved music, I couldn't seem to find the words to share with them my experiences in England — the theatres, the people and the audiences. The flat we lived in seemed like a place of strangers. Perhaps I should have stayed to help. Instead, I decided to leave.

My mother smiled and tried to understand, but her comments were really reduced to telling me that as long as I was happy, she was too. It took me many years to realize just what a wonderful thing her simple comment was and what a wonderful gift. It freed me from the guilt of leaving them; within days I had decided to leave. I was eighteen years old.

It surprised me to find that the other three Hollander Boys weren't as enthusiastic as I was when I suggested we go to Brussels and find another booking. They said they thought it would be better if I went on my own. I had the feeling I was being told that if I got a job they would be there — but they weren't going to suffer much anguish if I didn't come up with anything.

I have never been brash or full of self-confidence, but since music meant so much to me, I needed either to be determined about what I was trying to do, or I had to dismiss the idea. I had determination — even if it did have a close resemblance to youthful blind faith.

Brussels in the late 1920s and early 1930s was a city full of theatres and dance clubs and night-clubs where top entertainers from all over the world appeared. This was one of the reasons I had decided to go to Brussels. But there was another reason, something I can only call a premonition. I felt it had to be Brussels, and I knew that something was going to work out.

But for the first two weeks in Brussels nothing did work out. From the moment I arrived in the city I spent my time visiting every club I could find, and every hole in the wall that passed for one. Because the clubs were closed during the day, the only time I could get inside to see the managers was at night. I would spend most of the early part of the day wandering around finding where the places were, then around five I would start to make my nightly rounds. I would walk until about two or three in the morning. My legs ached and ached.

If you have one of those stereotyped pictures of night-club owners in your mind — short, fat, bald, scowling and chomping cigars — you are describing a mirror image of most of the men I met. And that image pretty well fits their mood too, because most of the time they were just plain rude to me, and often a little cruel. Some of them laughed in my face, and others simply told me, in the vernacular of the day, to get lost. I suppose I can't entirely blame them. Here I was, just a kid who had never worked in a club in his life, trying to sell an act that involved a kid's instrument — with three of the four members of the act missing. Who'd ever heard of the mouth organ in a night-club, anyway?

It was discouraging, but every day a voice inside me told me not to give up. Sometimes that voice was a little weak, because there were a couple of things that came close to changing my mind for me. To begin with, I was running out of clubs in Brussels. At least, the kind of club I could work in and not get killed.

The second thing was that I was running out of money. I was two weeks behind in the rent at my *pension*, and I had the equivalent of ten cents in cash to my name. And I hadn't had a full meal in two days. Up to this point my premonition about Brussels had certainly fallen flat on its face. But things were about to change.

I was friendly with a young fellow who worked as the night clerk at the *pension*, and that evening as I was going out he called me over. He asked me if I had been to any of the clubs outside the centre of town, and in particular he mentioned a music club called the Bœuf sur la Toit. I had never heard of the place, but decided that it would be my first call of the evening.

I had an extra long walk in front of me, so I started walking about eight o'clock to get there by ten-thirty. On the way I spent half my fortune on a big bag of peanuts, and all the way to the Bœuf sur la Toit I feasted on these roasted treasures. I had an awful stomach ache by the time I got to the club.

The English translation of Bœuf sur la Toit is something like 'Bull on the Roof'. Not too surprisingly, there was a large wooden bull on the roof. It was quite a narrow building, and it gave the impression that it would be tiny inside. But the front of it was still rather chic-looking, and it had an elegantly-dressed doorman standing outside.

I don't know why a Belgian nightclub in Brussels, with the French name Le Bœuf sur la Toit, should have had a doorman with a great flowing red beard, and a name like Ian Bartlett McTavish — but there he was. He was a very jovial man, who I later found out had the reputation of being one of the best known bouncers in the city. That was surprising because he wasn't that big a man. However, I was told he held the unofficial record in customer fling: three and a half bounces from doorway to kerb!

When I presented myself to him, he told me the owner and manager was a man called Jean Omer, and right at that moment he was inside. He said I would recognize him by the red rose in his lapel.

Inside, the entrance to the place wasn't very big or much to look at either, just a long, dim, narrow hallway. But when I got to the end of it I came into a large room that was very stylish and luxurious, full of lights, full of sound and stuffed with people. I spotted the red rose right away.

I don't know if I would go so far as to say that Jean Omer had a kind face, but compared to the operators of the other clubs I'd been to, I'd say at least he looked less like Al Capone. He was a short man, with very fine thinning blond hair and a pale, very round, face. All that saved him from looking completely washed out was the surprising ruddiness of his cheeks.

He listened patiently to my story about the boys in Holland and our tour of England. He didn't laugh or say 'Get lost!' And he didn't seem the type who would call McTavish to have me thrown out of the place. In fact, he hardly said a word. But have you ever had that experience of just looking into someone's face and knowing you like them? It was his eyes, of course — and his gentle grin. Finally, he turned to me and said, 'Sit down for a minute. I'm busy, but I'll be back in a little while. We can talk some more then. Have some hors-d'oeuvres.'

I cursed my bad luck because, apparently, the bartender had not heard Jean's offer of free food. I didn't ask for any though, I just sat there and listened to my stomach rumbling.

It turned out that Jean was busy because he had to go up on the bandstand. He grabbed a clarinet from one of the seats and sat in with the orchestra. A musician! I immediately

liked him even more. In all the years since then I have never
seen the manager of a club play with the band. Though I've
seen a few fire them!

For the next twenty minutes I sat there and listened to a
really good group of musicians. So good, in fact, that I
decided they were the best I'd yet heard. When Jean came
back it was obvious that he had been thinking about me even
when he was on the bandstand. He was very direct and said,
'Look, Max, I'm sorry. This is just not that kind of club!
People come here to dance and to listen to jazz. We just don't
have any place for novelty acts. Is there any other way I can
help?'

It seems funny that there I was, with a nickel and a few
peanuts in my pocket and no prospects, and yet I was so
excited by the band that the only thing I could think was
'Wouldn't it be terrific to play with those people?' I thanked
him and started to walk away and Jean said, in a very kind
way, 'Good luck, Max. Sorry I couldn't help.'

And then I turned around and blurted out, 'Could I play
just one song with the band?'

There was a long pause. He said 'Uh' a couple of times
and 'I don't know.' Then, without much enthusiasm, 'Yeah.
Wait here.'

Jean went over to the maitre d' and said something, and
then he went over to the bandleader who was on a break.
Then he came back and told me it would be all right with
the band, but that I had better play something easy and fairly
short. My mind went blank.

The introduction was done by Jean himself, who said
something about 'a young man from Holland . . . give a big
welcome to —' and there I was. I still hadn't told anyone
what I was going to play — to this day I don't know what
it was. But I do remember that it was something currently
popular, and that I started playing the tune by myself. Then
the piano and the drummer and the bass came in. Pretty soon
more of the band came in, as they got the mood and the
rhythm of what I was playing. Before the end of the number,
the whole group was accompanying me. And I was having
a wonderful time.

In some ways it was like *déjà vu* — as though I was back in Liverpool, playing that very first time with Jack Hylton. Except this was even better. This band loved jazz!

At the end of the song I jumped down from the bandstand, waved at Jean Omer and, a little light-headedly, made my way to the door. Although he was calling after me, I didn't hear him. The next thing I knew he had me by the arm and was saying, 'Where are you going, Max? Listen to those people! They like you!' And for the first time I was aware of how much applause there was.

'Come on back. Play something else,' said Jean.

And I forgot I was hungry. I forgot I had a stomach ache. I forgot I was down to my last nickel. Right then, I could have died happy. But the best part of the night was yet to come. An hour later, Jean Omer offered me a job.

At first I thought he was talking about a job for the group, because I had come in there to sell the four Hollander Boys. But then he made it very clear (and wisely so) that a harmonica quartet was not the thing for me. What he offered me was a weekend of work, which in night-club terms is Friday, Saturday, Sunday and Monday. He proposed paying me more money than I had dreamed about. The equivalent of all the money I owed the *pension* for the last two weeks' stay, and three hundred and twenty dollars on top.

As I tell this story it has the ring of a fairy tale. It isn't — though Jean Omer turned out to be a very steady fairy godfather. I stayed at the Bœuf sur la Toit for a whole year.

There is no better way to learn your art or craft than by practising it, and I had the chance to practise mine all seven days a week for the next three hundred and sixty-five days. I would start my working day at seven or eight in the evening, and end it about five or six in the morning. I don't recall ever being tired.

I loved Brussels, although much of the time during that year I hardly had any sense of being anywhere in particular because I seemed to be working all the time. Even my social life revolved around people who worked in clubs. After we closed, around four or five or six in the morning, large groups of us would gather in our favourite restaurant —

musicians, waiters, waitresses, kitchen help, bouncers —
and we would talk and have our own little party until about
a couple of hours before noon. Occasionally, if one of the
big-time jazz men was in town, we would gather and have
a jam session. I can recall several of them lasting until two
in the afternoon. It was an upside-down life.

The only time I had which could pass as a normal family life
came during the following summer. My mother and my sister
came down from Amsterdam to Brussels to visit me for two
weeks. It was the first time in over a year that I had spent any
time with the family. Also, as Xaviere was getting on for nine
years old it was the very first time in our lives that she and I
were really able to talk. The best time was when the three of
us took day trips to the beaches of Ostend, a seaside resort
sometimes referred to as the 'côte d'Azur of the North'. Not
only were the beaches lovely, but there was a sense of luxury
and occasion about the place itself.

The sea along the beaches at Ostend, and some of the other
coastal towns in Belgium, is so shallow that bathers have to
walk out an enormous distance before they can swim. So in
those days swimmers were picked up in pony-drawn carts,
and after about ten minutes, with the water level sloshing at
the pony's undercarriage, they were let out.

At the back of these carts there was a small compartment
which could be screened by a drape, like a shower curtain.
I could change in there on the way out to the deeper water,
but it really came in handy when I came out of the water. I
would start off the return trip a little wet, tired and cool, and
I could just pop out on to the beach completely dry and free
of sand. I loved that trip. It turned out that my sister was
more interested in feeding the ponies than being on the
beach, wet or dry. And my mother spent most of the time
sitting on the sand under a huge hat. I could tell that she was
very proud, and thought her son a huge success.

Life in Brussels continued to be good for me and I prospered.
I learned about trust there. I never had a contract with Jean
Omer — I never missed a performance and he never missed

a paycheck. But, beyond that, he didn't treat me as someone who worked for him and made money for his club — he treated me as someone he cared about. And he taught me a great deal about the public, and the business of working hard and not just putting energy into your performance but putting yourself into your performance too. He taught me about sound and balance and harmony. I went to him a musician and I came away a performer. And when it was time to go he encouraged me: although the two of us regretted having to part.

Some time earlier Johnny Fresco, a friend from boyhood who had formed a successful dance band, had come to visit me at the Bœuf sur la Toit with one of the members of his band. They suggested that I join their band for an engagement at a large dance palace in the Hague. So the first place I went to after Brussels was back to Holland.

It was the first time in my life I had played in front of an audience in Holland, and the first time I had been on stage in front of my father. He seemed very happy. But, as I spent more time with them, I saw that both my father and my mother appeared much older, and somewhat dowdy and a little frayed around the edges. I realized that the time I had been away had not been easy for them. I resolved to send them money in the future. When I spoke to my father about it he was terribly embarrassed, and shook his head back and forth saying 'No, *no, no.*' He only agreed when I told him it was simply extra money I had, and that it could be used for things that Xaviere needed and to buy Momma the odd present.

We both knew the truth, but it saved us from those terrible feelings my father must have known — of failure and needing help. I wish that at those times in my life I had had exactly the right words to be able to tell him that needing help is not failure, that his son would always know he was something special, and that I would treasure every moment we had spent together.

But my time in Holland wasn't all filled with serious thoughts, there was lots of fun, too. I must have seen and eaten with every relative I had in the country — and there were dozens of them. After the war there was only a handful left. How quickly happy memories blend with the sad ones of your life!

It was a warm family time, though I can't say that it was very memorable playing in the Hague. But I decided anyway to follow along to the next booking of the Johnny Fresco Band, because they were headed for Ostend. The money was really good, I liked the people, and I was toying with the thought that maybe Ostend would be just the kind of working holiday I needed. I already had my sights set on the step after that.

One of Ostend's attractions was its casino, where aristocracy, major industrialists and the just plain rich of Europe came to gamble for high stakes. But it wasn't the gambling which attracted me, it was the fact that some of the most celebrated acts in show business appeared there.

The Johnny Fresco Band was booked into an exclusive little night-club, which was just across the street from the big casino. They served only the best champagne, and there was a cover charge which would have bought a small chalet in the Alps. But very often it was worth it.

The club opened at eleven at night, and the band was supposed to play until six or so the next morning. We had been booked in as the house band, which meant that we played while the patrons sipped their Dom Perignon, or danced around the tiny floor, and then around midnight the featured act would come on. This was generally a very big name — and at those prices it had to be a very big-time player. So, as we were checking into our hotel, I asked the club manager who the player was going to be. He laughed and for some reason answered me in English.

'Ah, Max', he said, 'it will be a great surprise for you! He is a man of great stature.'

With the limited amount of English I knew, this caused me to expect someone tall. It turned out to be Coleman Hawkins. Coleman wasn't very tall, but he was still a giant. Here it is, over fifty years later, and if you are a lover of jazz you know that name and know that sax!

We stayed there for six months. And night after night I

heard and played with a parade of great jazzmen. And just across the street, at the casino, the big bands were playing — people like Teddy Stauffer from Switzerland, Jo Bouillon from France, and the great Ambrose and his orchestra from England. But it is the players from the black bands that I remember most. Not necessarily those with famous names you would know, just players in the group. But as the saying goes, 'They could make their horn talk to you!'

I learned so much, and I began to feel like a real jazzman. Not one of those musicians ever made me feel that they were looking down on me because I was young, or Dutch, or played the harmonica, or because I wasn't from London, Paris, New Orleans or Chicago. The only thing that mattered was the playing; and if you were good, that was the language which really mattered. I have always loved being around musicians. But it is not only because they make great music — they make great friends too!

In the category of people who were both great musicians and great friends, I would have to include Johnny Fresco and Karel (Charlie) Dikker. They were not just good friends, they were also crazy.

We had been in Ostend for about four months, and Johnny Fresco had been saving his money religiously so that he could buy himself his first car. Then he saw the car he wanted: a 1936 two-seater convertible. It was painted a startling yellow with great whitewall tyres and a couple of extra tyres at the sides, in the fender wells. It was also the type of car that had a seat outside, where the boot at the back generally is — a place Henry Ford called a rumble seat. It looked sporty, elegant and fast. Johnny took every cent he had saved and bought it on the spot. Unfortunately for Johnny, he hadn't taken the trouble to learn how to drive first.

After about a week, Johnny was getting very fed up with having the car just standing there at the kerb in front of our hotel, so he turned for help to Charlie Dikker, who was the drummer in our band. In 1936 Charlie was the only one in the entire group who knew how to drive, so Johnny decided that Charlie would be the one to give him driving lessons.

For some reason I was invited along for the lessons —
either to provide moral support, or ballast in the rumble seat
at the back. On the first day Johnny seemed less than eager
to start, but bravely he turned the key and the motor hummed
to life. He swung round to me, sitting in the seat outside,
and said 'Are you you all ready to go, Max?' I said yes,
though in truth I wasn't sure. there was a look in his eyes
you might see in those of someone falling off a building —
and I noticed that the sweat from his palms was soaking his
driving gloves. Johnny let out the clutch and stalled. 'That's
it,' he said, 'I'm not ready!' On the first outing we had gone
only ten feet. But if you think Johnny wasn't ready to drive,
you should have seen how ready Charlie was to teach!

If the old saying 'Them as can, do, and them as can't,
teach' is true, then Johnny Fresco would have qualified as
a full professor. After six long lessons the only thing left for
Johnny to learn was starting, steering, stopping, and keeping
some balance between his driving speeds — which seemed
to continually fluctuate between nine miles and sixty miles
per hour. On the seventh such lesson, after making a vow in
my heart that this would be the last nail-biter — I took my
place in the rumble seat and off we went.

Johnny started off at his usual safe speed of eleven miles
per hour for the entire time it took to get us out into the
countryside. Charlie (who was never particularly patient),
suggested that he would walk ahead and meet us later.
Johnny seemed to take the hint and speeded up. And up. And
up. Soon we were both yelling at him to slow down, but he
seemed frozen at the wheel. I remember we were racing
down the road parallel to a railway track, and I had visions
of us coming to a crossing and banging into a train head on.
I leaned forward and put my head in my lap. Charlie must
have had some kind of vision too, because suddenly he
stopped yelling and started to kick Johnny's frozen foot off
the accelerator. Then he grabbed hold of the steering wheel
and banged on the brakes. I was thrown forward in the
rumble seat and its lid slammed shut. I was stunned.

Then, from the muffled distance of the front seat I heard
a voice say, 'Oh my God . . . we've lost Max. He's fallen

out of the damned back!'

I could hear the car doors open and slam when the two of them changed places. And, while I was still trying to regain some of the air that had been pushed out of my lungs, the car wheeled around and skidded off back down the road. By this time I was banging on the lid, but they couldn't hear. It took them about two minutes to realize that the rumble seat lid was down and that I just might be inside.

They often asked me to come along for another lesson, but I never did. Then, about three weeks later, Johnny sold the car. I am positive that many people are alive in Belgium today because of that sale.

It was during that stay in Ostend that I had met Ray Ventura. As well as having his own orchestra, he had a very large and important talent agency in Paris. He suggested that, if I would telegraph him when I was coming, he would set me up with a place to live in Paris. Well, I did telegraph him, and when I got to Paris there was a Dutch-speaking man waiting for me at the railway station, with a large car to take me to Ray's office.

After we had chit-chatted for a couple of minutes Ray said, 'I think you had best join my band for a couple of radio broadcasts to begin with.' He took out a huge wad of money and handed me a large pile. 'This is for the first week. Oh, by the way, I've got you a really nice hotel to stay in. It's on me.'

4

Personalities in Paris

MY TIME IN Paris was remarkable not only in terms of my career, but also because of the people I met. I don't know how it is that I have had so much 'people luck' over the years. Show business is supposed to be tough and you are supposed to watch your step. Well, I never had a contract with Ray Ventura; and I've almost never had one with anyone over my whole professional life (except when it was required for union reasons or for corporations like the BBC). And I never once got stung in anything that mattered.

Ray's radio shows were very popular, and he liked to have guests. That's how I met Maurice Chevalier.

When I first met Maurice he was a big star in France and I had just joined the Ray Ventura Orchestra. I can remember that sometimes a group of us would stay on in the studio after the broadcast, and sit around with some bottles of wine and play for our own sheer enjoyment. When Maurice was on the show he would nearly always join us — singing, laughing and being very witty as he did a play on words with the lyrics or made them naughty. It wasn't quite a jam session — that wasn't Chevalier's style of music — but it was spontaneous and fun.

Though we didn't talk very much, I still gained a very strong impression of his personality. Physically, he was tall and slender. He had a long and rather crooked nose, as though he had been in at least one fight where he had come up a loser. All of this was put on a long face so French in character that it could have been designed as a national symbol. And then, of course, there was his trademark; a lower lip which protruded slightly and gave him a pouty

our-year-old Max with his mother and father.

Max and his father at Zandvoort beach, Holland.

'Mac' Geldray and his Mouth Accordeon Band, 1934.

Max (far left) with the Johnny Fresco Band.

Playing harmonica with Ray Ventura listening in. Paris, 1937.

Jam session at the Hot Club de France, 1934, with Django Reinhardt (on guitar)
and Duke Ellington (standing, centre). Max plays harmonica (middle, right).

Max, second on left, 'Le formidable soliste' himself!

Max's sister, Xaviere, around 1942.

The car that saved Max's life in 1940.

Max on drums, Kees van Dijk on accordeon and Jimmy Kirk on harp in the army band, 1941. Max still keeps in touch with these friends.

look. But, inspite of the crooked nose, pouty lip and long face, you wouldn't help but think of him as immensely handsome. I don't know whether you would call it magnetism, a strong aura, charisma or sex appeal — whatever the contemporary term is, Maurice Chevalier had the quota for about three men.

Part of it lay in the way he gestured and moved his body — broadly, smoothly and in an almost feminine way. The movements were so expressive it gave you the feeling that he was choreographed as he talked. And then of course there was his smile! Chevalier had a very radiant pink complexion, and his smile made his eyes light up. When he looked at you, it made you feel as though you were being rewarded with total and affectionate attention.

The truth is I wanted to be like Chevalier (and he is one of the few stars I have met in my life I would say that about). It really didn't have much to do with the fact that he was rich and celebrated; I just wanted that shine.

My last meeting with Chevalier came when I was on tour with Ray Ventura and we were in Brussels. By this time, Maurice had risen from being a French star and a European celebrity to being an international superstar. He had been to Hollywood to make feature films, his recordings sold world-wide and he could go and work anywhere around the world and be recognized. It was late morning when Ray telephoned my hotel room and asked me if I would like to go to lunch with him and Maurice.

An hour later the three of us left the hotel in a taxi, on our way to a café that had been recommended to Maurice. It was a small place in one of the quieter districts in Brussels, and Maurice had made the reservation. When we got to the street where we were supposed to have lunch you could not even see the front of the building. The street was covered with hundreds of people.

In those days Belgian middle-class businessmen were a very formal group. They were profoundly aware of their dignity, and to suggest that you would see one outside his office without his tie on and his jacket buttoned was fantasy beyond possibility. Here on this street were a dozen such

men — coats off and ties askew — as though they had just
run out of their offices. And there was a sea of other people,
too: children, old men with canes, shopkeepers in aprons,
young girls with flowers in their hands, and every other size
and shape of female. It was a very impressive tribute to
Chevalier that in their excitement these conservative
Belgians had forgotten, so quickly, their public etiquette.

Obviously, the proud owner had spread the word that the
great Chevalier was honouring his establishment, and the
news was known throughout the entire district.

When Maurice got out of the taxi there was a hush, and
then a loud burst of hurrahs and applause. Beaming, he
turned in a complete circle and waved at his fans. It is
interesting that they didn't crowd in on him, but seemed to
give him room, as though they were showing deference to
his specialness, something that doesn't seem to happen very
much today.

But not everyone in that crowd was deferential or shy.
Suddenly, from out of the pack came a huge bulk of a
woman, wearing a shop apron over the top of a great flowery
housedress. She rushed forward and wrapped her arms
around Chevalier and planted a big, smacking kiss, directly
on his lips.

Maurice may have been surprised, but he carried the scene
off with great panache. He took her hands in his, gently
raised one to his lips and, with the other hand, held her palm
directly over his heart. The oohs and aahs and applause were
thunderous. The lady stood there transfixed. Her eyes
glazed over. She was in sexual shock.

When we got inside the café, Maurice wiped his lips and
said, with a great wide grin on his face, 'Why are they never
the beautiful ones?' He did not say this in any sense to
ridicule the woman, but in a style that was charming and
raffish: a style that was his signature to a world-wide public.

As far as women were concerned, the truth was that easily
half of the beautiful women of Europe would have traded
places with that Belgian housewife. And, at that point in his
life, it sometimes seemed as though Maurice was trying to
fit them all in.

Years later, after the War, Maurice Chevalier was condemned in some quarters for having collaborated with the Nazis. I don't know whether or not it was true that he had. Some of his friends have told me it was not; that he was ordered by the Germans to entertain them, and had no choice in the matter.

The Germans carefully sought out people like Chevalier as much for their propaganda value as for their worth as entertainers. And there are supposed to be many pictures of Chevalier standing with the Nazis, as though to give them public approval. But I find it difficult to believe that this man, who loved France so much, would have co-operated willingly to curry favour with the Germans.

Many years later I saw him on the screen in 'Gigi' and there it was — that same quality was still there. I still believe he was something special in everything he did.

Another person I met at that time, whose reputation has endured, is the man who is still reckoned by jazz guitarists to have been one of the best ever: Django Reinhardt.

It always surprises me that any reputation should last so long. After all, we are talking about a man I met in the 1930s, who has been dead since 1952. Django played jazz in Paris at a time when the whole jazz field was dominated by Americans. And he played the guitar at a time when that instrument was really off the mainstream of jazz. But then I suppose I shouldn't be surprised, because Django was so original and so damned good. As I sit here, remembering us playing together fifty odd years ago, I can honestly say that I have never heard anyone better.

Although it was very hard to tell his age, I would guess that Django Reinhardt was not yet thirty when I first met him in Paris in the early part of 1938. He had already gained himself a large local reputation in jazz circles by playing the guitar at the Hot Club de France. The guitar wasn't featured very often in jazz — most of the time it was just a background rhythm instrument — until Django Reinhardt came along.

I had been playing the harmonica for almost five years,

and had been in Paris for about ten months. I was being billed as a 'special attraction' on Ray Ventura's radio shows. It was almost impossible not to make a reputation with that kind of exposure: we were doing four broadcasts a week from Paris, three for the French network and one for Radio Luxembourg. In those days the Ray Ventura Orchestra was considered to be the king of bands in Europe, so by the time I met Django he had already heard about me.

Django was of medium height with a Latin type of dark, swarthy, good looks. The craze in Paris at that time was apache dancing, so Django's macho good looks had a special appeal to the French and the French ladies. The very dark complexion came from the fact that Django was a gypsy, and his family had probably originated somewhere in the Eastern part of Europe.

The boyhood years of Django's life were led in the traditional gypsy nomadic style — wandering across the Continent in a horse-drawn caravan. In fact, until he was eighteen, Django had never slept anywhere but in a gypsy wagon, or under the stars. He had never gone to a formal school, had never lived in a house, and there was hardly anyone in his entire family who had a job, or stayed in one place for more than a few weeks at a time. It is little wonder that there was a kind of 'move on' spirit in Django throughout his life.

But to understand Django's world a little better you have to understand how gypsies were thought of in the mid-1930s. The words 'gyp' and 'gyp joint' come from the word gypsy — for they were a people with a reputation as thieves and scoundrels. In those days, even children could tell you that gypsies were not to be trusted. They were said to appropriate every chicken in sight, and to steal children as their caravans passed in the night.

Another part of the gypsy reputation was built on the fact that they were mysterious wanderers, given to fortune-telling and thought to be able to cast evil spells and curses. The superstition and the prejudice led to gypsies being outcasts: and quite a few of this independent, nomadic people preferred life that way.

In fact, most gypsies were simply travelling families going from place to place shoeing horses, selling pots, helping to plant and harvest the crops, selling phony religious artefacts and charms, and of course setting up their wagons for their fortune-telling. If they lived by their wits, it was because they were pretty shrewd observers of human nature. By the time Django was six he was pretty shrewd himself, and he was doing almost every one of those gypsy jobs — except maybe shoeing horses.

By the time I met him, most of the gypsies had had to curtail their wanderings, because Germany was like a huge stone wall across the face of Europe. Adolf Hitler and the Nazis had decided that gypsies were a threat to the Aryan people.

I seem to have mentioned all the things that made the public mistrust gypsies, but there were areas where they really were appreciated — one of which was for their music. I don't suppose there are many people who haven't heard the expression 'gypsy violins'. There *is* a true gypsy sound though unfortunately most of us associate it with the schmaltz of a tune like 'Golden Earrings'. But the real root of gypsy music, and the sound of those gypsy violins, is in something called the Hungarian gypsy scale, which is actually made up of two scales. It is a very limited and a very stylized musical form.

The instruments the gypsies played most often were violins, guitars, tambourines and a kind of gypsy flute. You might think that because Django knew no life but the gypsy's world, complicated by the fact that he had a badly mutilated left hand, he would have played his guitar in the traditional way that gypsies played. But not Django.

When Django was about twelve years old, there was an accident in camp one night. A fire had started in one of the caravans and Django joined the others in trying to put the fire out. Suddenly a gas lamp exploded and the flames shot out and Django was terribly burned on his left hand which was left deformed, with very little movement outside the thumb and first two fingers.

While he was recovering, an uncle gave him a present of

a small guitar. Perhaps it was a present in honour of his bravery. Perhaps it was to help his crippled hand. Or maybe simply because music and dance were so naturally a part of gypsy life and culture. Whatever the reason, it turned out to be the most significant event in Django's life.

His brother Joseph told me that, after just a few weeks, Django was making sounds and tones that were extraordinary — rhythms that no one else in the tribe could even come close to. All this dexterity, feeling and virtuosity from a man with a deformed left hand! As Joseph said, 'From the moment he picked it up, it was almost as though he was born to play it!'

But it is still hard to understand how jazz entered his gypsy world. And no one seemed to be able to tell me why Django loved jazz, or where he developed that completely non-gypsy musical skill. I once asked him, but he never did answer. He just shrugged.

Django and I first met at the Hot Club de France. With a name like that, you might assume it was a jazz night-spot, but it wasn't. The club was exactly that: a place with a business office, books and magazines, the latest news on who was in town, who was playing where, and where to go for the after-hours jam sessions when the other clubs in Paris had closed down for the night.

Very frequently I would arrive at those offices and find a jam session in progress there, and that is how I first met Django. There were about six of them playing some light melodic jazz and after I had been sitting there for about fifteen minutes, one of the musicians asked me to play along. After the session had broken up Django came over to me and said, in his very husky voice. 'Tomorrow. Four. Vin Blanc Café'

It was rather a terse invitation, but the next afternoon I was there. Django was sitting in a small back room by himself, and the only thing he did was nod at me. Then, without a word, he started to pick idly at the strings. I took my harmonica out of my pocket, thought of a tune and started to play.

We played for about two hours. Occasionally we would

stop for a sip of wine and look at each other and smile. But
we hardly spoke, and we never commented on what we were
playing or how we were playing it. Finally he got up from
his chair, looked at me and said. 'Next time!'

Because music is an experience in itself, it is very hard to
describe those sweet moments and Django's specialness. I
find myself reaching for superlatives to describe him, and I
know that won't do. Perhaps it is better merely to point out
that I am talking about someone whom musicians and jazz
aficionados revere to this day. A man who was at the peak
of his artistry. Django's guitar was so expressive that at
times it was like a human voice crying out the pain, the joy,
the hope and the exhilaration of the music. All the sounds,
whether they were in a slow lament or a flurry of notes, were
extraordinarily clear and perfectly fitted together. I
remember that during those hours, when there were just the
two of us together, it was often very difficult to keep on
playing. Half of me wanted to stop and listen, while the
other half was feasting on these moments of playing with a
great player.

Django and I would often run into each other and find
ourselves 'jamming' with some other musicians. I was
working exclusively with Ray Ventura, so we never worked
together professionally. But that hardly mattered, because
we still had those occasions when we played for ourselves.
Always it would be the same: the two of us in the middle of
the night, with a little wine, a little talk and much music.
Some time in the dawn we would simply part, until chance
brought us together again.

There were long periods when Django would disappear
from sight. There didn't seem to be any particular reason or
cycle to it. Django's brother, Joseph, once told me, 'Django
is a gypsy! That is the reason! One day he will not come
back.' But Django always did come back, until the end of
his life. Django may have been a gypsy to the core of his
soul — but Django needed jazz. And jazz people too!

Up until the time I left Paris, in 1940, I would see Django
on the street. Most often he was shuffling along, shabby and
unshaven, looking like someone down on his luck. His

guitar hung carelessly over his shoulder, as though he were some second-rate street musician. While Django was never very prosperous — he would work steadily only when the spirit moved him, or if he needed money to pay his debts or to buy a few presents for the ladies in his life — it is still hard to understand this curious 'between engagements' behaviour. When he worked in front of an audience, it was like a metamorphosis. He would be stylish and immaculate, and even his guitar would seem to have been polished. But Django never played any better to the most glittering audience than he did on those nights we spent together in an empty café.

At the beginning of 1939 there was continuous discussion and argument in Paris about what would happen next. A great many people thought the whole prospect of war was an impossibility. They insisted that the First World War had taught the Germans a lesson. They said that the Maginot Line would dissuade the Nazis and that France and England were just too strong for Germany. But, as the early months of that year passed, there was no doubt that we were hearing more and more about war, and less and less about peace. And whether you were a peace-thinker or a war-thinker, you felt the tension around you rising every day.

At that time I was travelling with Ray Ventura's Orchestra all around the country, and everywhere we went we could feel the short temper of the people and see the strain in their eyes. Yet, strangely, I don't recall that anyone I met mentioned any plans to pack up and leave, or said that they were thinking about sending their children away. And most of the show-business people around me seemed to be just ignoring the whole thing, as though our private world somehow protected us against the world outside.

But there was one thing we couldn't ignore completely: the steady flow of refugees.

In both 1937 and 1938 there had been a growing stream of them from Germany. Not just people who were politically opposed to the Nazis, but a long list of others: artists, writers, comedians, musicians, scientists, intellectuals, gypsies, homosexuals and, of course, Jews.

We had no hint of the extent of the concentration camps. Extermination camps were not yet hinted at. But there were many stories of people losing their homes and possessions, and of others simply being taken away in the night. Taken somewhere.

I had heard stories about the treatment of Jews and gypsies — stories of beatings and children taken from their families — but there was no picture of what was going on: just fragments of the crimes.

What we did know was how formidable the Germans would be if we roused them. The Nazis took every opportunity to photograph and display their barbarity. In the film newsreels we had seen them march and bomb and gun the countries of the east and the north . . . Austria, Poland, Norway. They had carefully shown us all their symbols: black uniforms with skulls, swastikas, jackboots with clanking iron heels, the massive rallies and fanaticism, the screaming bombers and bombs. They were meant to show the world that they were a tide, an unrelenting, unmerciful and invincible tide. And here was France on the brink of war with them. When I think about it now, I can see that the Germans were very clever in preparing us for defeat.

In the autumn of 1939 I was barely into my twenties and my life was full and rich and good, so it is no wonder that I kept on listening to the voices that promised peace! And, as far as my family was concerned, it was also a great consolation to me that Holland was once again a neutral country.

Then war was declared! It seems that no matter how much you expect it, when it comes war creates immediate chaos. There was much shouting in the street about how we would beat the Hun, but even then it seemed more of a self-assuring bravura than bravery. Almost immediately, the French government ordered foreigners out of Paris. It was a strange order that affected every foreign national whose country wasn't in the war on the side of France. I have no idea what threat I was supposed to be to France. Some I spoke to put it down to the fact that it is a national trait in the French always to harbour a slight suspicion of foreigners. Perhaps that had something to do with it.

The French government allowed us foreigners a little time to pack up and make plans for resettlement. And none of the other Dutchmen, Belgians, Americans or other neutrals seemed in any hurry. There was no real war front in that autumn, and beyond the fact that the border between France and Germany was closed, there was hardly any feeling that the country was at war. No guns, no bullets, no dead. But I decided to leave Paris as soon as possible, because I felt the need to go to my parents.

I had never been the kind of devoted son I thought I should be. It wasn't that I had ignored my family, but my attention over the last few years had been infrequent, sometimes half-hearted and often given grudgingly — as though I were performing a duty. The only thing I had done regularly was to send them money. It was never very much. Perhaps not even as much as they needed. I think this was the first time in many years that they came first in my thoughts. Deep in my heart, I felt they were in the path of the war — and they were Jewish.

I had a new car, a Citroën, and the very next day I simply said goodbye to everyone (as though I might see them in a week or two), packed some of my things, and set off. I planned that my larger possessions, and my memorabilia, should be sent to Holland by truck. You can see, it wasn't much of a war!

5

Fleeing to Freedom

I DROVE FROM Paris into Belgium in wonderful autumn weather. I had driven through that countryside many times, and in the pleasure I took in it I could almost delude myself into believing that everything was normal. When I came up through Antwerp to the border with Holland my mood changed.

I had crossed between Belgium and Holland at that border point literally dozens of times. These were two neutral and friendly countries in a non-fighting war. But evidently they had set up some new rules!

One quickly learns that all governments at war, or living in the shadow of war, move inexorably in two directions at once. First, the bureaucrats develop new rules — which are hard to defend and, sometimes, just plain mindless. Second, the bureaucracy begins to move at a new pace, one that would compare favourably to the latter stages of rigor mortis. And when and if it does move, it moves nervously.

The new rules I found at the border had to do with my car. The Dutch wouldn't let me take my French car across the border into Holland. 'Why?' I asked. 'Because it is the rule.' That was the only answer I ever got.

It wasn't very far across the border to Amsterdam, but I had the feeling that the car might be necessary as a way out for my family. Indeed, later, it was to turn out to be exactly that for me.

Since I was determined not to give up that car, I headed back through Antwerp and directly south to Brussels. I thought that perhaps I might be able to talk to authorities in the capital and straighten the whole thing out. Whether this was the right solution or the wrong solution, it was the only one I could see.

When I got back to Brussels I found, to my amazement, that the city was almost unbelievably calm. Those who read the newspapers or listened to the radio must have been reassured that no war would ever be fought. Oh, there were the Cassandras who spoke of the danger, but the loudest voices said, with great assurance, that a declaration of peace was about to be made. I met some old friends from Holland, and they too seemed to think that things would work out. I remember one of them said, 'We're neutral, Max. Anyway, what would Hitler want with Holland?'

I couldn't phone my parents in Amsterdam, because there wasn't a single phone in the whole of the apartment building in which they lived. So I wrote them a letter, asking them to write back and assure me that they would be safe. Then I spent a few days trying to talk to the authorities in Brussels.

No matter whom I talked to, the story was the same — I was not going to get my car across that border. The most encouraging words I heard were from an old gentleman, who told me that things would change 'after it quietened down a bit.' I didn't have the heart to ask him when *what* quietened down.

I can only believe that the bureaucrats were simply confused by the thought of war, and feared the consequences of everything they did — anything which might displease either warring side.

It was even more apparent to me that there was great logic in keeping the car with me. If peace was about to be declared I could use the car to see my family, and then return to Paris. If there was war, there was nothing but bicycles for us in Holland. And where would we go?

Over the next few days I met some of my old friends from Holland and Belgium, and I began to feel much more secure. Jean Omer, my old boss from the Bœuf sur la Toit, had opened a second club and he asked me to play there. When Jean and I talked about things, I was buoyed up by his 'Forget about the war! Forget about the Germans!' But somehow I couldn't. Time passed and I played every night at Jean's club. The world should have seemed normal and comfortable again, but somehow it didn't. It was at this point that I met Lili.

I have mentioned that one of the notable features of some of the musicians I worked with was that they were jokers. Practical and impractical jokers. I had never been known to wear a lampshade at a party, tell ribald jokes or drop my trousers that is, until I shared a room in Brussels with a drummer friend called Martin. And Martin was a joker of overwhelming proportions.

It all began when he came home one day and announced like a bolt out of the blue, that he was going to marry an old girlfriend. It seemed he had bumped into her on the street, and he now realized he could not live without her. It surprised me because I had never heard him talk about her, and I'd known him for perhaps four years. He said it was going to be a small, informal wedding and he asked me to be his best man. He then handed me a ring, a simple gold band, and instructed me to be at a church on the other side of the city at two the very next day. I must have asked him six times 'Are you sure you know what you are doing?' He nodded each time.

After Martin had left, rushing out of our room saying something about arrangements, I was still left gasping for breath. I might have grown suspicious, except for the fact that later on a couple of his friends strolled by. They mentioned that they too had been surprised to hear of the wedding, and we talked about it for a long time. The trap was sprung!

The next afternoon, like a dutiful dolt, I went to the church, still more than a little disturbed that my very dear friend was getting married so hastily. When I got in the door I immediately saw the bride-to-be. Her name was Lotta, and she was a very gentle and quiet girl. So it surprised me when, after I had given her a very big smile, she asked in a loud voice what I was doing there. I said, 'I'm the best man!'

'You're the what?' asked Lotta. 'That's going to be a surprise to my fiancé!'

'Aren't you going to marry Martin?' I asked, with a
sinking feeling in my heart.

'Yes, I am! Martin, do you know this man?' said Lotta.

I turned and, of course, he didn't know me. Her Martin
wasn't my Martin.

There were several men waiting outside the church on the
pavement, obviously enjoying the scene of me slinking out
of the church. They kept chanting over and over, 'Are you
sure you know what you are doing?' I resolved that revenge
was vital, or I would never have any peace from Martin.

I was searching under the bed for a shoe when Martin
announced that he was going to bring a couple of friends
home to play poker. I was glad I was looking at the fluff
beneath the bed and that my face was hidden from his view,
for a look of supreme evil must have crossed it. It was time
to set my snare.

To prepare myself for Martin's return, I fluffed up my hair
and put something on my head that looked like a Miss
America tiara. My lips were slightly reddened, my eyes
slightly darkened, and my beard for the day slightly shaven.
I then dressed in high heels and a large red bow — placed
strategically over my manhood. The rest was left bare and
hairy.

I could hear footsteps in the hall, so I gathered up my only
other prop and took my place behind a curtain. The prop
was a small sign which read 'Your bride!' Then, when it was
turned over to the other side, it read, 'And too good for you,
too!'

The door opened and I popped out. There was Martin with
his two friends. They didn't say a word, but just stood there
with their mouths open. One of them smiled sweetly and
said 'Nice!' Then she and her friend turned round and
walked out.

I sent the lady poker-players some flowers soon after that
and a note of apology. But they didn't respond.

Not long after that I was working in the club and saw some
friends of mine sitting at a table with a large group of people.
I went over and was introduced all around. One of the people
at the table was called Lili. Lili, of course, turned out to be

one of the young ladies at my bridal party. She said 'Ah, yes, Max Geldray. We've seen each other before!' That night we started our romance.

If it was a strange beginning for Lili and me, in many ways it was also unusual that we were attracted to each other at all. She and I were very different from each other, both in our backgrounds and our temperaments. Lili was from Brussels and came from a very wealthy family. She was sophisticated, extremely well and expensively dressed, and had the kind of style and haughtiness you might find in a model from *Vogue* magazine. It was almost a cold stylishness, and she brought to it a tongue and a temper that were sometimes fierce. She was certainly attractive, with a very small, round face, which was quite beautiful. She was also voluptuous. But I think the reason I was drawn to her went beyond her being so attractive and different from most of the women I had known.

Before this trip to Brussels, I had been living in Paris for quite a while. I had celebrity and money, I was living in fine hotels and eating good food and I was invited to an endless round of parties. And I had very few obligations. By the standards of a great many people, I had it made. It is strange that this was the point in my life when I felt that something was missing.

In part it may have been the stress of the war, which does many things to people, things we don't necessarily associate with the war itself. I hadn't had a real home life or a family life since I was sixteen. It may have been that I just wanted to focus my affection on one person. I think Lili needed me in much the same way as I needed her — as a kind of emotional blanket. Something to cover our uncertainties and fear. I know I was not in love with Lili, but she held a very strong attraction, and many of our moments together remain as cherished memories. Whatever my reasons, in a matter of a week we were living together.

Nowadays it is so easy to say 'we were living together', but it was a different world in the 1930s, and as a rule men didn't find it easy to persuade women to climb into bed with them — though for some reason it seemed to be comparatively easy for musicians to do so. In spite of that, before Lili, I had never let any of the women in my life move in with me. The truth was that I had never yet felt I needed anyone enough to want to dedicate myself to her.

It was after Lili and I had been living together for about two months that some of my old friends, musicians, from Amsterdam showed up at Jean Omer's club. The next afternoon we met for lunch on the patio of my hotel, and after much laughter and wine we decided it would be a grand idea to have a musical reunion. It turned out that my three friends had a small musical combo and were booked to appear at a club in Antwerp. They suggested that Lili and I join them there. Both Lili and I had been to Antwerp separately many times before, and for each of us it was a city of pleasant memories. So we agreed to go along and meet my friends in Antwerp the very next week.

Antwerp lies about fifty kilometres from the Dutch border. It is a seaport, lying on the Scheldt River in the northern part of Belgium. In the late 1930s, in spite of being a port, it was an attractive place. I don't think you would have called it an exclusive spa, but it was a place you could go for a plain, old-fashioned good time. And in the late spring of 1940 the weather was clear and warm, by Belgian standards, and the river not too cold. The hotel we booked into was crowded with people who were older than we were, a sort of upper-crust crowd of sunseekers, but they were a great deal of fun to be with.

As for the club I was working at in Antwerp, it turned out to be quite pleasantly different from what I was used to. It catered to an older crowd. It was more like a rather staid old dance-hall than a jazz club. And so, for the first time in a long time, I found that I wasn't playing all through the night. Instead I began my day at six o'clock and finished at midnight. I felt as though I were on vacation. It was not only a very healthy life, it was a daytime life. And that was a first for me in five years. I even became an early riser!

It was on one of these mornings when I had leaped out of bed almost as the sun was getting up, that I was attracted to the window by some loud noises: noises that sounded like a

steady heavy thumping of thunder in the distance. The sky
was completely clear. But in the distance, about two miles
down the coast from the hotel, I could see puffs of white
smoke rising up from the area of the waterfront, an area
where I knew the docks were located. I woke Lili and we
walked out into the corridor and found it crowded with other
guests. Many of them were running around in confusion,
asking over and over, 'What is happening?' I wouldn't
describe it as panic, because I am sure that no one there
thought of this as war. Why would they think that? Every
day the Brussels newspapers were full of reassuring
statements. Over and over you heard 'The Belgian
government is confident that the Axis nations and the Allied
nations will come to some form of peace agreement'. The
Belgians had the peace of mind that comes with neutrality
— and the French were between them and the Germans.

From the hallway we could see that there was a steady line
of people making their way up to the roof garden, so Lili
and I decided to follow. When we got there, we found there
was already a crowd of nearly a hundred people: guests
dressed in everything from elegant formal morning wear, to
people in their pyjamas, housecoats or swimsuits. Even in
that crowd it wasn't hard to see what was happening, but it
was hard to make any sense of it. We were looking into a
beautiful clear, sunny morning, and we could see more and
more puffs of white cloud rising from the area around
Antwerp harbour. And we could see many large aircraft high
in the sky over the harbour.

It seems odd, and terribly illogical now, when I remember
what we thought at that time. The consensus on the roof was
that the planes were from strong and mighty England. I
remember the Belgian gentleman next to me saying in a loud
voice, 'It is the English! They go to get the Germans!' We
were instantly convinced that the Royal Air Force was
flying over Belgium on its way to bomb the Germans. The
puffs of smoke were from the anti-aircraft guns. Of course
the Belgians, as proper neutrals, had to shoot at the British
as they invaded Belgian airspace. But, as this same man
observed, 'Look, see how they miss!' After this comment

there was some scattered laughter at the charade.

There are two possible reasons for our naïvety. First, what did any of us know about war, especially war from the air? Secondly, under severe stress I suppose even the most logical among us can make ourselves believe that what we don't want to be true isn't true! (In my own work today with those suffering from one form or another of chemical dependency, I would call that 'denial').

Suddenly the planes seemed to be spreading across the sky and approaching directly over the city. At that moment a porter in a white coat came flying up the stairs, shouting, 'The Germans are bombing Antwerp!'

I can remember that the only thought which came to my mind was simply, 'No. *No!*' Lili and I just stood there with the others — just stood there — watching the bombers, which seemed now to be moving in our direction. At last they came so close that we could see that shiny objects, like metal balls glinting in the sun, were falling from the sky. And when we looked up from the horizon we could see that the bombers had spread out over the sky and that some of them were now almost directly overhead. Then bombs began to explode just a short distance from the hotel. The Germans had more than the harbour in their sights.

There was something about the hotel staff in Antwerp that was both admirable and hard to believe. They were so well-trained and disciplined that, even as they found themselves surrounded by falling bombs, they were concerned about the welfare of their guests. In just a few minutes they had several hundred of us down in the cellar of the hotel. We listened to a radio station which seemed to come on the air almost at the moment the bombs had ceased to drop. We were told that the harbour was in pieces and that many people had been killed. They also warned that more raids could be expected. And very soon after that, the hotel above us began to shake again. There were two more raids on Antwerp that day.

It was about six hours after the final raid that we heard that the Germans had simply ignored that impenetrable bastion, the Maginot Line, by simply going around it through the Low Countries. Holland, we were told, was either falling or had fallen.

In the confusion of war a great deal of the information one gets is misleading, contradictory and just plain wrong. One tends to believe the worst. I could not contact anyone in Holland; I could not even find my Dutch friends in Antwerp. In fact I found it impossible to locate any of the people I knew in Belgium. So Lili and I decided it was time for us to move and react in response to the rumours we heard . . . and the panic we saw. One piece of information was certain. The Germans were headed for Belgium.

Lili and I went down to the dining-room of the hotel, where everyone seemed to be furiously gulping coffee and discussing their plans to get out of the way of the approaching war. Lili and I decided that the best thing we could do was leave Antwerp for Paris. Immediately!

Since we had only come to Antwerp on a working holiday, most of what we owned was stored at Lili's apartment in Brussels; it took us perhaps half an hour to pack the few things we had brought with us. Just as we were ready to drive off toward the Belgian border we were approached by three men. I had met them a few days earlier at the hotel and we had struck up a conversation; it had turned out that they were in the diamond business in Antwerp and, when I told them that my mother's family was in the same business in Holland, we had discovered that they knew several of my relatives. Now they asked if they might join Lili and me in our flight out of Belgium.

In the late 1930s, not everybody had a car; in fact, there were many people who could not drive. And here was I with a brand new car. I am not sure I can claim that I took them along for humanitarian reasons. Perhaps I thought about safety in numbers, or just had the urge to get it settled and get out of there. Whatever the reason, in a matter of minutes they were packed shoulder to shoulder in the back seat, their small valises jammed in to the boot with one of my bags left to its fate on the lawn in front of the hotel. To this day I cannot recall the names of these men or much about what they looked like, beyond the fact that they were in their late forties or early fifties. And that is strange, because for the next little while we were very close comrades in war. And it may be that one of them helped to save my life.

I mentioned that Lili and I were planning to go to Paris; perhaps I should have simply said France. We had no plan — not even a final destination — we simply thought we should get out of the way of the war . . . a war which was now sweeping through Holland and Belgium on its way to encircle France. I remember we did have some discussion about getting across the border into Spain, and I don't doubt that fully half of the refugees in France and the rest of Europe had the same idea.

We decided that if we were going to avoid getting involved in traffic jams (on roads crammed with cars, trucks, wagons and almost everything else that moved on wheels) and possible air attacks, it might be a very good idea to keep off the main roads. And it turned out to be a very good strategy, for there was very little traffic on the minor roads and, beyond a few burned-out hulks and the odd hole in the road, there was very little evidence of the war. But it turned out that there was one very large complication.

The German High Command had been very methodical. Not only were they meticulous planners, they were also leading the only nation in Europe prepared to fight the first modern war. And they had made their plans well in advance. In 1938 a German company, which manufactured a very famous brand of facial soap, had begun to put up roadside advertising billboards all over the Belgian countryside. Now it was discovered (and I don't know how) that covered over on the back of these signs were maps of the countryside, with strategic military and resource facilities carefully and fully marked in.

The Belgian government enlisted the army, civilians, farmers, children, almost anyone they could find, to tear them all down. At the same time they ordered all the other road signs across the country to be taken down, so that the advancing Germans would have no help. Getting across Belgium on the back roads was, at times, like solving a puzzle. We zig-zagged. We lost our way. We measured distances on the map and read it off our odometer as though we were measuring distance in feet. We timed our distance. We lost our way again. But we didn't dare stop and ask some nervous farmer — spies were reported to be everywhere.

It may be a short drive from Antwerp to Brussels by the direct route, but it took us well over five hours to get to the outskirts of the city. Our next shock came when we stopped for food and were told that the Spanish had closed all their border points with France and that Switzerland was impossible. And we were also told that even the border between Belgium and France was a nightmare. Lili came very close to deciding to stay in Brussels; after all, we were just ten miles from her apartment and from some of the members of her family. In the end she decided to continue on with us. But I don't think that decision had much to do with me or our relationship. I think, like myself, Lili just wanted to get away from war and the Germans.

We were about to leave Brussels but I had stopped at a garage, so that I could have the car filled with petrol, and Lili and one of our fellow-travellers could find a shop and buy us a good supply of food. While we waited at the car, I got into a casual conversation with the man at the petrol station and began to talk to him about our trip across the country. I asked him whether or not there had been bombings or sabotage around the countryside, and told him about seeing burned-out cars and trucks on even the side roads and that there were surprisingly few cars and almost no people to be seen. The reason, he told me, was that the German *Luftwaffe* was using Stuka dive-bombers in a very un-dive-bomber way.

It seemed that these small, gull-winged Stukas were capable of flying at incredibly slow speeds. He told me they could actually stay in the air when doing little more than fifty miles an hour. The tactic of the German Air Force was to fly their Stukas very low and follow trucks and cars along the highways. When the plane was directly overhead, and travelling at the same speed as the vehicle being pursued, a small bomb would be dropped directly onto the roof or the bonnet. It wasn't that they were particularly interested in blowing up a car and killing a few people, their real purpose was to create panic on the roads, and in this way keep them clear. And it certainly did deter many travellers. The Nazis were not worried about meeting resistance, they were worried about meeting their timetable. It was this information which probably saved the lives of all of us in that car.

I cannot remember what point on the border we were headed for, but it seems to me now that, on the French side, it was fairly close to Lille. We were travelling along a two-lane badly-paved road, approaching a T-junction where we would turn on to the highway which was about two miles from the border. The traffic had been getting heavier and heavier in the last hour and suddenly we found ourselves stopped in a line of it. We were parked there for about two hours and at last I got out of the car and walked ahead to see what was holding us up. What I saw was a solid line of cars stretching about two miles in front of me up to the junction, and then another mile or so beyond that was solid with cars stretching as far as the border. I didn't count the cars, but there were hundreds.

We seemed to be parked on that country road for ever. About once an hour we would move up one car length. Occasionally a large military vehicle would pass down the other side of the road. Once, when a vehicle pulled out of line, a large military truck came down the opposite side, honked his horn to show his impatience, and then simply pushed the car off the road into the steep and deep ditch beside us. The car-driver and his wife screamed in despair, but there was nothing anyone could do to help them get the car on the road again. The last time I saw them they were walking, carrying their luggage and food, toward the border with France.

Occasionally, as we sat there beside the car, we could hear air-raid sirens in the distance, and the people around us spoke in whispers — as though speaking out loud might draw the *Luftwaffe*'s attention. We heard stories of other border points being bombed, of cars being blown up and hundreds killed. And here we were, exposed like sitting ducks. We were to remain there for over two days.

The countryside around us was fairly flat and bare, the only shelter to be seen was a small wood that covered one corner of the junction ahead of us. A junction where we could turn right, back into Belgium, or turn left into France. We moved toward it at an agonizingly slow pace.

Suddenly we heard the sound of sirens wailing from the border just in front of us. People jumped out of their cars, and ran for the cover of the trees. The sirens went off four more times that day.

By the next day we had advanced in the line until we were at a point almost directly opposite the wood. We were heartened that, at last, we were only a mile or so from the border, and had the chance of making it before any more planes arrived.

But then the traffic movement seemed to stop — and we sat in that one place without moving for hours and hours and hours. By the time we had been at the border for two days we were out of food, desperately tired from the tension, and aching from sleeping in the car or on the ground beside it. We needed supplies of food and water, but obviously couldn't move our car. We decided that each day two of us would start off well before dawn to walk the six miles back to a small village because, fortunately, there was still plenty of food available all over the countryside. But we decided, mutually, that otherwise we would not leave the car.

Throughout all of this time Lili had been very composed, and I think that her strength made each of us feel a little braver. It wasn't that she made light of our predicament, but she was so optimistic and self-assured that we felt certain we would not only make it to France, but go safely from there. Then something minor happened. Something that should have meant nothing. But, in those times of stress, it was enough to change our relationship for ever.

Given the right circumstances people can come to know each other intimately in almost no time at all. Lili and I had known the men in the back seat for only a few days, and yet there was a strong bond among us. Yet even if, in most ways, our behaviour with each other had changed, in other ways it hadn't.

There was that small area of woodland just ahead of us, and whole families had moved into its cover. They used the place to cook, to sleep and, though it was about as private as a public ward in a hospital, as a latrine.

We had decided that when Lili had to relieve herself, each of us four men would take a blanket and hold it up in front of her. We would form a square, creating a sort of tent without a roof. And it worked — although I know it was embarrassing for Lili to make the request.

Once the four of us were holding our blankets when suddenly the air-raid siren blasted, and almost immediately we could hear the sounds of aircraft in the sky. The three back-seat gentlemen dropped their blankets and headed for the ditch. I just stood there stupefied — with the blanket held in place. Slowly Lili's head appeared over the top. With great tenderness she looked at me and said, 'Max, you are the bravest man I have ever known!'

I stared blankly at her for several long moments, and then — I couldn't help myself — I began to laugh. I laughed and doubled up until the tears ran down my cheeks. I didn't hear the sirens, or the planes as they passed away. Or anything else for that matter.

When I finally looked up, Lili was gone. I found her sitting in the car. After that she very seldom spoke to me, and the affection I had grown used to in her voice had disappeared. I wanted to tell her that I wasn't laughing at her, or ridiculing her sentiment. I wanted to say to her that, after all the tension and fear, it was as though a dam had burst inside me. I wanted her to see the ludicrousness of it all: that here we were worrying about her showing her bum, when all of us might have our rear ends blown off at any second. But I couldn't find the words at first; and when I did she would not listen.

On the fourth day it seemed as though we were inching ahead a little more quickly — and then I heard someone say that the border might be closing. The rumour flew that when we got to the crossroad we would find ourselves turned in the opposite direction, away from the border. We kept telling ourselves it was just a rumour — but our tension grew.

There was a light drizzle throughout the day, and every-thing was getting damp and wet; the car was steamy inside, and the fields around us soggy underfoot. To make it worse, by this time the road had very curiously narrowed, so that as we got closer to the corner, hugging our side of the road, we found ourselves perched on the lip of the ditch. Though the car had to rest at an uncomfortable angle, it was better than having one of the trucks come along and push us off the road.

On that fourth day I had reached a pitch where I felt it was time to either get across that border or leave this place for ever. I decided on a plan. I told Lili and the men that the next time the sirens blew they were to run into the woods and keep on going until they reached the border. I said, 'I'll get the car there.'

It was less than an hour later that the sirens sounded again, and everyone ran for the trees. But I stayed behind and started the Citroën. I pulled on to the other side of the road and gunned the car toward the crossroad. Almost as soon as I had turned left I found a car blocking my side of the road. I pulled round it and swept into the ditch. I thought for a moment that I would tip the car over, and slide into the deep mud in the field. But I didn't.

To this day I bless that Citroën — and the marvellous front-wheel drive that kept me perched on the side of the ditch like a mountain goat. In two minutes I had reached the border point. The gate was down, but whoever was in charge was lying low inside the shelter of the building.

When the all-clear sounded people came out of the building and out of the woods, and I could hardly believe that no one asked me how or why my car had suddenly appeared near the head of the queue. I have no idea why no one did. Perhaps everyone was too preoccupied with their own troubles, or simply too emotionally drained to bother. In a few moments Lili and the three Belgians came walking up to the car, and within half an hour we were being processed by the border guards.

In the years following that day, I have often thought that perhaps we were cowardly to push ahead of the others that way. But then I remember the feeling of being desperately vulnerable . . . and the continuous flutter of panic that it produces. That border was a very potent symbol to everyone there. Although if we had thought very clearly we would have realized that the Germans were perfectly able to bomb both sides of the border.

Indeed, when we got to the other side people seemed so much more secure that there were even cars waiting there before beginning their journey into France. Someone at the border had told them that if they travelled in convoy they had a better chance, presumably because of breakdowns and wreckage on the road. We joined four other cars for about the first hour and then I took my Citroën and put the accelerator to the floor.

You could feel the tremendous relief in the car, but still we had no sense of security. The three men in the back seat were constantly looking out of the side windows and through the back, scanning the skies for any sign of aircraft. Lili, in the front seat beside me, leaned forward so that she could see ahead and above for any signs of the Germans. No one talked. We flew down that road to Paris and I kept having to tell myself to slow down and conserve our petrol.

Occasionally we would see a bombed-out car or truck, and once there was a bus, shot full of bullet-holes, with at least two bodies lying by the side of the road. There was only one man at the scene, and he was sitting on a stool as though he was waiting for a bus. When we stopped to talk to him he waved us on impatiently and wouldn't say a word. Lili had never driven a car, but at one point I had to ask her to lean over to my side and steer. My fingers seemed to have grown completely numb.

It was mid-afternoon and we were on a long straight stretch of road, with only an odd tree on either side to give us any cover, when one of the men in the back seat yelled, 'Look out!' and the car filled up with shouts. It was only by instinct that I pulled the car to the wrong side of the road and jammed on the brakes. We all rolled out of the car and into the ditch beside us. In the next few seconds we heard a rapid pop, pop, pop — and then heard the bullets hitting the road. I looked up, and there was a Stuka.

The German pilot was flying so slowly and so low that, as I lay there on my back in the ditch, I could see his head through the canopy. He was flying down the centre of the road, and as he got within what seemed like yards from the car, he pulled the nose up sharply and stopped firing. Ahead of him there were large trees hanging over either side of the road, so he banked the aircraft into a very tight turn. For a second the plane shuddered and seemed to hang in the air motionless. The engine howled and then, as it grabbed the air, it jerked forward. He barely missed the trees.

I got up and ran over to the car and drove it into the trees — ignoring the ditch and the mud and the possibility of being stuck for ever. I was certain he would come back to finish the kill, but miraculously he flew away. My God, those Stukas were ugly planes!

In half an hour we felt safe enough to leave the trees and put the car back on the road to Paris — with mud and ditchwater on our clothes, but not even a scratch or a bullet-hole as a souvenir.

I don't know what kept that pilot from coming back. Was it because of his close call with the trees? Was it because the car was off the road and he lost interest? One thing I do know, if I had kept that car on the road, with my accelerator to the floor, we would all have been easy pickings for that Stuka.

I will always be very grateful to the man who told me about Stukas, at that garage outside Brussels.

We stayed overnight on the outskirts of Paris. During the night we decided that we should head for Biarritz, which was about three hundred miles away. After we got that far, we told ourselves, it would be easy to cross the border into Spain. We started off about four o'clock that morning.

The day turned out to be dismal and misty. The clouds were dark and heavy with rain, and yet as we drove into the day all that fell was a continuous light drizzle. By now the temper of all of us in the car had changed, almost as the weather had. While we had been on the edge of danger, waiting to be bombed or shot at, we had clung together. It seemed that then there was a sense of harmony among us, as though we had known and trusted each other for a long time. Yet now, when we had almost evaded the immediate dangers of war, our relationships seemed to turn sour. I had the feeling it was now 'everyone for themselves'. I suppose prolonged stress does that to people. It seems to operate on extremes, making you either close companions, bonded to one another, or strangers wanting to escape, and rip away from your memory every trace of the people and the time.

Then suddenly there it was, Biarritz, looking, even in the rain, like some bright and elegant sanctuary. Unfortunately, the first thing we found when we stopped in the city was that the Spanish had closed their border with France.

There wasn't much choice about what to do next, so we set off for the seaport of Saint Jean de Luz and headed for the harbour.

Saint Jean de Luz is a pretty place with a tiny harbour. It is also shallow, and the larger vessels must lie at anchor at least a half mile away from the dockside. When we arrived there we saw two boats anchored offshore in just that way. But the first thing that struck us was that the harbour shore looked like nothing less than an enormous car-park, with hundreds of cars and people milling about everywhere. We parked as close to the harbour as we could get, but in fact we were barely off the road leading to the harbour entrance. For a moment we thought seriously about turning round and heading somewhere else. But where?

Two of the men and I made our way to the dockside, and found out that the boats offshore were two British cargo vessels. We were told that they had been sent to Saint Jean de Luz to pick up the remnants of the Polish Army. Well, whatever the numbers they had expected to find, there were very few Polish soldiers at the dock.

We could hear people talking very excitedly to men in uniform who sat in front of the dock. It was obvious that many of them were wealthy and that they were trying to bribe their way aboard. The three men travelling with me had industrial diamonds with them, and they too tried a bribe.

The problem was that you did not know who the people you were attempting to bribe were — nor whether they had any authority and could help.

But I am sure that considerable fortunes passed from hand to hand that day as people tried desperately to find help to get aboard one of those ships. For whatever reason, whether they thought the diamonds were glass or didn't know their worth, our bribe didn't seem to interest anyone!

Lili and I, and the other three men, all felt despair that, after all our effort, we weren't going to escape. But, as long as those boats were out there, we weren't going to leave either. And it was fortunate that we didn't, because within the next few hours our problem was on its way to being solved.

It was well after four o'clock in the afternoon. Lili and the others had gone down to the dockside to be on the spot if there were any news about boarding the boats. I was sitting on the ground, leaning back against the car door. The mist and drizzle from the harbour was now so heavy it was almost like a fog, but it was somehow comforting — as though it would make me invisible to agents of harm. And although I was getting wet, I was very happy to be outside the car.

I had that terrible gnawing, nervous feeling you get in your stomach when you feel you really should be doing something and there is nothing left to do. To comfort myself I pulled my harmonica out of the glove compartment of the Citroën and began to play something very quietly.

It would be very dramatic if I could say that I sat there on the ground playing something poignant, like the 'Saint Louis Blues'. But the truth is that it was a long time ago and I cannot remember; all I know is that it was music with that melancholy feeling.

After a few moments I noticed a tall, lanky Frenchman who was dressed in the uniform of the French Air Force. He was just standing there, listening to my playing. Then he approached me.

'Is there petrol in your car?' he said.

'Why, yes,' I answered, not knowing whether, in these times, it was wise to admit to anything.

'If I had that car, I could get to an air base not far from here. I could fly my plane to England!' he said. 'I'm a fighter pilot.'

Now there was no possibility of my giving up the car, even for so patriotic a reason. And, frankly, I didn't know whether to believe him or not, so I said, 'If you can get my four friends and me on one of those boats you can have the car.'

He looked at me with a slight grin on his face and said, 'It is possible!' And off he went.

I don't know how he did it. Perhaps he spoke to the English captains and told them he was on his way to England with a fighter. Perhaps it was something else. However it happened, about an hour later he came back and told me, 'It's all set!'

The only condition to our getting on the boat was that we were to go to the dock one by one, and go rather discreetly. The ship's company wanted to avoid what might turn out to be a riot. When my new friend found out that there was also a female in our party, he insisted that Lili wear a man's hat over her tucked-in hair. The airman ushered all of us right up to where we had to jump into a little motor boat that would take us to the bigger boat, and then I threw the key of the car to him. I have often wondered if he made his trip to England safely.

At that scene there were hundreds of exotic and expensive cars to choose from. Why did that Frenchman choose my little Citroën? Did he pick me out because the Citroën was fast, full of fuel and parked near the entrance of the harbour road?

Or did the harmonica save our lives? Did it somehow draw his attention to me, and then spark something inside him? I swear to you that these events are true — it is only the 'why' I don't know. But I have to confess that the version where the music saved our lives is the one I prefer!

It was pitch dark when we climbed aboard that large

vessel and now it began to pour with rain. We didn't weigh anchor for hours because motor boats were now dashing back and forth, bringing more and more people from the dock. Somehow a decision had been made to take aboard anyone who had a desperate reason for wanting to escape.

I remember that when the engines began to throb loudly and we began to move slowly out of the harbour of Saint Jean de Luz, I went to the rail and put my head against it. I was utterly drained and exhausted, and my knees seemed ready to buckle beneath me. A man came up behind me and put his hand on my shoulder, saying, 'Max!' I turned and there was a cousin from Amsterdam I hadn't seen for five years. I now knew that at least one other member of my family had escaped.

6

Soldiers in Exile

ACROSS EUROPE THERE were millions of people in the middle of a terrible war, and many of them were starving, so I suppose it is only right that I feel a little petty and peevish when I find myself complaining about the food we had to eat on our voyage to England. But as we zig-zagged from the bottom of the Bay of Biscay to Liverpool, we had nothing to drink but water, and the ship's menu consisted of nothing but corned beef. I am not particularly finicky about eating corned beef — it was, after all, a kind of a wartime hero-food, which ranked right up there with Spam. And as Napoleon might have observed, it did help to keep Britain's military travelling on its stomach. But during the six days of crossing I seemed to develop a violent allergic reaction to it, and I broke out in large bumps. After the fourth day, hunger or no, I couldn't face another bite. And that, together with leaning over the rail in heavy seas, left me looking like something along the lines of tapioca in mint sauce.

There were about seventy civilians on the boat when we docked in Liverpool. The few Polish soldiers who had come on board were taken off in one direction, while we were herded on to buses and taken to a large hall in London. At first the scene was a nightmare: at least half a dozen languages could be heard, many of the refugees had no proper identification, everyone looked slightly ill and a great many were weeping. Meanwhile, the officials were trying to help these people find sanctuary in England, while also trying to ensure that none of them were German spies and saboteurs.

For the next three days, most of us lay on benches which

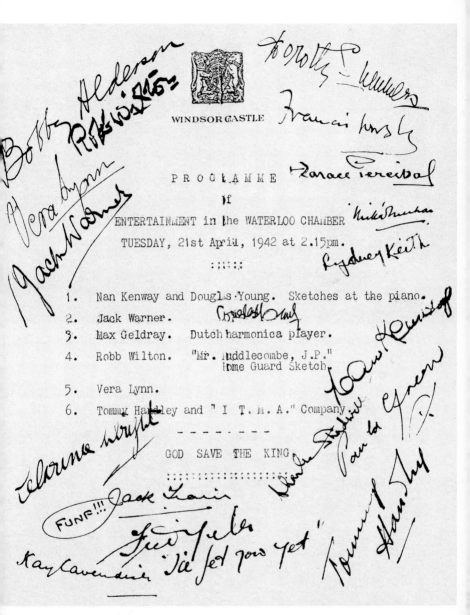

The programme, signed by all the players, from that memorable night at Windsor Castle, 1942.

The original Goons: Harry Secombe, Michael Bentine, Spike Milligan and Peter Sellers. Note the hair!

The Goon Show team, 1953. Left to right: Ray Ellington (whose quartet featured in the show), Harry Secombe, Spike Milligan, Max Geldray and Peter Sellers.

The legendary Ella Fitzgerald and Max appearing in Cardiff in the early sixties.

Jamming with Peter Sellers and Sophia Loren at Peter's home in Elstree in 1960.

Strongman act. Spike Milligan, Max Geldray and Peter Sellers in Variety.

Clowning around again ... but whose is the extra arm?

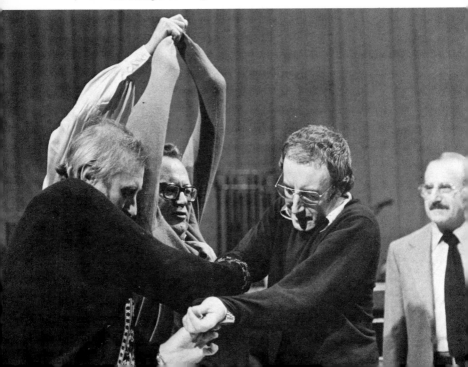

lined two of the walls, all of us sleeping fitfully and never feeling rested. I think all of us felt we would never find the days long enough to give us the sleep we needed. Then someone would come in and take one of us away for an interrogation. That seemed to happen at least four times a day, and last for anywhere from twenty to thirty minutes. Our interrogators weren't harsh or threatening, but they asked the same questions over and over.

At other times, when I was awake, I sat in a stone-faced solitude in a corner. For the first two days I don't suppose I said ten words to anyone in that hall. But then the mood of the place began to alter, and some of my tension slipped away. The crowd of people was changing — some were being sent on their way, while other refugees were appearing from other boats. The questioning was still going on, but now I found it much less stressful; I thought I could feel an unspoken assurance that no one was going to be turned away.

During this period I saw my cousin two or three times, but I never saw Lili or any of the three men she and I had travelled with.

Years later I found out why I had not seen them. It was when I met a man from the very hotel we had been staying at during the bombing at Antwerp. This is the story he told me. Long before the war the German High Command had methodically planted hundreds of spies in the cities and the countryside of Belgium. Shortly after the first bombing, some of those spies were now certain that the invaders would be there in a matter of days. So, very brazenly and quite openly, they started to ask questions. In fact, we had hardly left that hotel before there were people enquiring about the men in the back seat of my Citroën. My Belgian friends were then put on a most-wanted Gestapo list. We were being hunted — and would have been shot on the spot — because it turned out that my three travelling companions were known to be carrying a rather large bagful of industrial diamonds.

There is an old folk saying: 'What you don't know, won't hurt you.' In this case it was certainly true.

Now the British didn't believe that anyone bringing a
wartime present of industrial diamonds would be a German
spy, so the three men were whisked through customs — with
Lili in their midst. Somehow I was left at the gate. I never
saw any of my diamond-merchant friends again. Or Lili
either.

But I didn't have to stay at the gate too long either. I had
told the officials that there was a man in England named
Leslie McDonald who could easily identify me; he was an
agent I had met in the days when the Ray Ventura Orchestra
was touring England. They got in touch with him at about
the same time they discovered I had helped the men with
the diamonds. Talk about a door-opener! A smiling
immigration man turned to me, almost tipped his cap, and
said, 'You can go, lad!'

Of course they didn't simply dump me on the street, they
provided me with a chaperon. I found myself travelling in
the company of a tall, unsmiling man in civilian clothing. It
was obvious that he didn't speak any Dutch, French or
Flemish, but that was no worry because I spoke enough
English to more than get along. However, I couldn't for the
life of me follow anything that he was saying. To this day I
can see him standing there, staring into my face about eight
inches away, speaking at me in the very loud and precise
way one addresses extremely inattentive children — or
someone who is not only foreign and un-British, but also
stone deaf. Since that time I have become aware that he was
a Scot. It wasn't until I had lived in England for about two
more years that I could finally follow what Scots were
talking about. And then I married one!

My lodgings turned out to be in a part of London called
Fulham. I suppose it could then have been described as
lower middle class and a bit run down, although I don't think
anyone would quite describe the house, or the district
around it, as shabby. My Scots guard rang the front doorbell,
and a small slender woman popped the door open and said,
'Ah, you're here!' Feeling rather giddy at this point, I was
tempted to shout, 'No we aren't!' But instead I smiled
blankly.

There was a quiet dignity about this lady, even though she was dressed in a creased cotton housedress and had a red kerchief wrapped around her hair. And there was great warmth and comfort too, when she looked at me and said, 'Make yourself at home, lad, I'll put on the tea.' Home sweet English home!

Most public patriots are heroes because they are noticed doing the deeds. Sometimes, in wartime, they are simply chosen from the pack to become symbols — to provide the kind of popular inspiration that makes us all a little more serious about the job. As far as I know, my new landlady was never a symbol to anyone, but I came to think of her as a kind of private patriot — a symbol of why Britain survived that war.

I am reminded of her every time I see or hear the actress Maggie Smith; not only was my landlady called Maggie, but in her face and voice she was very similar to her.

She had a husband, a son and two brothers away in the army. She worked a great deal of the time in a factory to aid the war effort. And, together with a very ancient aunt, she ran a boarding house for dislocated strangers like myself. Every time I entered the kitchen she seemed to be busy knitting socks and preparing packages for the boys. It was the kind of tireless endurance I couldn't believe in a woman with that stringy slenderness.

My room was on the second floor and it was small and sparsely furnished. I suppose it might have been described as gloomy, because it had just one tiny window that looked out on to the brick wall of the house next door. But it was marvellous. The landlady's tea was always tasty, and strong enough to get your attention. And she herself became like an aunty to me. In her home I instantly felt safe.

When I think of that house now, I can remember that there was always the slight odour of gas from the gas heater. Although it is like a combination of sulphur and cooking cabbage it is a smell which I find comforting even to this day. Maggie, the aunty and the house aren't there any more. They were all blown up at the height of the blitz. I have imagined them sitting in the kitchen drinking tea when it happened — I think that is a very English way to go.

On my very first day of freedom in England I was given a large pamphlet to read, which spelled out all the rules of conduct while I was the guest of the country. The Crown would pay my rent, and give me an allowance for food and necessaries. There were only a few restrictions on my life: I was to observe a night-time curfew which would keep me off the streets after eleven, report to the office where I had been processed in seven day's time, and I was admonished not to be loud or drunken in a public place, since this would make the British public think unfavourably of my nationality. There was one other rule I found out about that was serious — and it wasn't in the pamphlet.

At the end of the seven days I went to report to the authorities and found out that I could not get a work permit of any kind! They said they would continue to give me money for the rent, and a small allowance to live on. It was poverty living, but very generous of the Crown. However, they didn't explain what I was supposed to do with myself.

I don't think anyone could have explained that to me, because at that point I don't think anyone in the government knew what to do with refugees. The tide of people escaping Europe meant great numbers of people, quite suddenly, dropped on the British doorstep.

Jobs were out of the question. Nor did they think it a good idea, or quite the time, to take young foreigners into the British army. And they certainly had no intention of putting us in an internment camp, as the Germans were doing. So we were put on a shelf. I had much time to wander the streets of London and observe the British.

In that first part of 1940 London was not really a city at war. It is true that there were hundreds of people in the streets wearing uniforms, and that we could feel the bustle of preparation and a momentum building up for the war. Certainly the radio and newspapers were full of it. But, except for the faces of the people I met who had come back from Dunkirk, London was showing only smiling faces and slight signs of war.

Even as the streets were darkening more and more with

practice blackouts, the pace of life was still normal and carefree in London. I remember going down a street and walking past the pubs at closing time, and seeing Londoners crowd out on to the pavement — jolly, singing, arms around each other. And I thought to myself, 'You don't know what you are in for! You think it's a lark. Wait until you get bombed!'

That was peevish of me. Of course, when the bombs started falling, I was the one surprised. The English are a stalwart people. And if deep inside they were tormented — grieving at the loss of so many of their young people and apprehensive about the conduct of the war — it hardly ever showed on the outside. They remained warm and laughing and brave. Throughout all those years I kept seeing and hearing that British brand of optimism. Backed into a corner, they are the most 'everything will turn out all right' people on the planet.

During this same time the shifts in my own mood were rapid and contradictory, and often without any noticeable cause. I felt relief at being safe and the excitement of being in London, then waves of loneliness and despondency. And I found myself becoming resigned to the fact that my parents and my sister would not make it through that war. I am not a fatalist, but I sensed they were lost to me. I sensed this in a way that I have sensed several important happenings in my life.

During those first few months in London I did not meet any other Dutchmen or refugees. My life consisted mostly of walking London streets and sitting morosely in my room. My landlady was my only friend, and it was she who suggested that I had to get my life started again. So I decided to see some of the people I had met when I had toured England before the war. The very first person on my list was Leslie McDonald.

I had first met Leslie in 1937, when he had brought Ray Ventura and his orchestra to England. By anyone's definition, Leslie McDonald was a very prominent promoter of major musical events in England. When I arrived at his office I was shown straight in by his secretary, and I was surprised to find that he was on the telephone talking to someone about me.

'But damn it, man, what's he going to do while he's here?' Leslie was obviously very exasperated. 'Look, he has worked in England before. He's not some damn Nazi on the sneak. We have to help this man. How's he supposed to eat? What am I supposed to do, break the law to help someone who has escaped the Germans?'

There was a lengthy period of silence in the room, with Leslie obviously listening to a long speech from the other end.

'Please, Matthew,' said Leslie, in a voice full of quiet frustration, 'see what you can do!' And he hung up the phone.

'Max,' said Leslie, 'I've made about a dozen calls and it doesn't seem to matter how many strings I pull. I'm damned if I can get you a work permit!' He turned and looked up at me. 'I want you to go over and see my friend Harry Roy. If we can straighten out this work permit he will be the first one to help. Here's his number. See him!'

Anyone who ever talks about theatrical agents being a hard-hearted group should have met Leslie McDonald. And anyone who thinks of the English as cold-hearted should have met Harry Roy.

For quite a few years, going back perhaps into the early 1930s, Harry Roy had been a big-time bandleader in England. I had known about him in Holland, and even collected his dance-band recordings long before I was a professional musician myself. I was flabbergasted at the prospect of meeting him. So, the very next day, I took some time out from my very unbusy schedule and went off to see Harry Roy.

He lived somewhere close to Park Lane in an apartment that, by anyone's standards, was posh. The carpet wasn't merely thick, it was more like wearing a second pair of socks. And when I sat on a couch it was like being in free-fall, right up to the point where I felt I might disappear. Since both Harry and I were slight, and not particularly tall, we had sunk almost out of sight by the time we started to talk. The decoration of his living room seemed very modern, and today would probably be called Art Deco — I don't know what it was called then. We sat in it for about a minute and a half and then went to sit at the kitchen table.

Over a brandy Harry Roy told me that he couldn't do anything about a work permit, but he did offer to introduce me to some people, and, as he said, 'At least get you invited round.' Then he asked, 'Max, did you bring many of your things with you?'

When I replied that I had got out with very little of anything, he took me into another room and opened up the doors of a very large clothes cupboard. Inside was enough clothing to fill the dress requirements of seventeen people in four climate zones. Harry was a clothes-horse! He smiled, waved his hand and said, 'Well, help yourself. Really! You can see I've got enough.' I was looking at about seventy-five suits. But I didn't take one. It certainly wasn't that he couldn't spare one, or that they wouldn't fit. The truth was that I was so touched by his generosity and friendship, that I felt that by *not* taking one I was somehow giving him something in return. I know that doesn't make much sense, but he had given me a much greater gift. Friendship!

These had been truly lucky times for me in England; new-found friends in Maggie, Leslie and Harry, all in the matter of a few weeks. The funny thing was that, after I had left Harry Roy, the day turned out to be an even luckier one.

It began on a London bus. I had left Harry Roy and had been walking the crowded streets for a long while. By now it was late afternoon, and the clouds were building up so that the sky was beginning to look like night. I thought to myself that it was time I was getting back to my boarding-house, to have tea with Maggie, so I boarded a bus and was sitting by the window on the left-hand side, next to the pavement.

If you have ever been on a London bus you will know that they are noisy contraptions. Add a crowd of passengers, and it is unlikely you will hear anything from the street. I had been watching a very pretty girl who was sitting across the way when, instinctively, I turned my body right round and

looked out of the window behind me. I thought I had heard
a voice calling out something which sounded like my name,
my Dutch name: Max van Gelder. And there, on that
crowded street, was someone waving and running along far
behind the bus.

At first he was so far behind me that I couldn't make out
the face. When I could see him, it was like a dream. Here in
London, in absolutely the wrong place, were the waving
arms of one of my boyhood friends. His name was James
Grootkirk, though he was known in London by the more
English version of Jimmy Kirk. What are the chances of his
walking down the right street at the right time and seeing
me on a crowded bus? You can only believe it was meant to
be!

Jimmy had been a friend of mine since those first days
when my family moved to Amsterdam. His mother had been
a concert pianist before the war and he played jazz harp and
saxophone, so the thread of music ran through our
friendship. It had led to my spending untold hours at his
house.

But there was more to this event than finding an old friend.
I knew that the Royal Family of the Netherlands was in exile
in Britain: Queen Wilhelmina, Princess Juliana and her
husband Prince Bernhard, and their two little daughters the
Princesses Beatrix and Irene. What I didn't know was that
this government in exile was about to form its own small
army, the Royal Dutch Brigade. But Jimmy did! Within two
days Jimmy and I made our way to the Dutch Embassy and
joined an army in exile.

On the 20th day of September 1940, I was officially
inducted into the Princess Irene Brigade, and was sent off
to camp. The camp was made up of large tents, perched on
the side of the sea in Wales very close to the seaside resort
of Llandudno. There were only a couple of hundred of us at
first, looking well-tailored in our new uniforms, but not
much like soldiers. There were several rifles in camp, but
most of us carried broom handles or long sticks as we
marched and learned the disciplines of the army. We felt
quite proud of ourselves at times, although perhaps a little

sheepish when we had to take our turn at guard duty defending the coast. I suppose, through an exercise of sheer will, we could have beaten an invader senseless with our sticks! But there was something that was even more disconcerting than having sticks for guns.

The Germans were making propaganda broadcasts directed at the Dutch in Britain, and occasionally we would listen because there would often be news about Holland in their reports. Sometimes there would even be a mention of specific people in the families of one of the soldiers. Then they started to put other things into those reports as well. Thing's about us! Describing us and our broom-handle guns. And, in a very good-natured way, giving us such details as the camp clock being two minutes slow.

It was a ploy which was supposed to tell us that all was forgiven, to go home, the Brits weren't our friends. And it was supposed to tell us that the Germans were everywhere, and that we had better be suspicious of all the Dutchmen around us. Here we were, ready to defend the coast, and the Germans knew everything but our latrine habits! But it is interesting that eventually the propaganda had the opposite effect on almost all of us. When the Germans talked of their superior power and their hold on Holland, it made us yearn for revenge. It made the enemy real.

It was about eight weeks before we all had rifles and began to feel like true soldiers. We moved around the country to several other camps, then settled down near Wolverhampton at Rothersly Park, as a camp for the Princess Irenes was built around us. By now our numbers had swelled to several thousand, but there still wasn't much action.

To overcome their feelings of loneliness the boys would get together and play cards or, for a really exciting evening, go and see a film at the camp cinema. However, despite the training and the waiting, and the training and the waiting, I wouldn't describe those times as dull, not with the arduous drilling we had to do every day. But it is true that the most exciting times we had involved an enemy we never saw. Almost every week seemed to find ourselves out in the storm-lashed landscape, searching from dawn to dusk for saboteurs. There were constant reports that they were being dropped by parachute. Our job was to capture them and stop them from disrupting the war effort. But we never encountered any saboteurs — although we did run into the odd chicken and a few loose vegetables in a field. These were taken back to camp for questioning.

It was in the early part of the spring of 1941 that I was sitting in the barracks at the Dutch Brigade base. About an hour before we had been on a particularly exhausting training exercise and I was sitting in a chair wondering whether my body would ever again feel as though it liked me. One of my friends came into the room and told me that there was a message that I was to report to the office of the Base Commander. That was not a very unusual thing to happen, because quite often I would get a call and find out that the dance band I'd formed with Jimmy Kirk had been requested to play somewhere. The Brigade always bent over backward to accommodate the Royal Air Force or the British Army bases. The High Command felt it was very good public relations for the Dutch.

But the reason for my being called was not about music, it was about Holland. When I got to the office there was a man standing by the doorway in civilian clothes. At first I didn't recognize him and, when I did, I could hardly believe he was there.

Seeing someone unexpectedly in wartime is quite different from peacetime for it is an instant confirmation that they are still alive! And this alive man standing before me was a long-time acquaintance from Amsterdam named Jaap Sajet. I had met Jaap when we were both young boys, and he had played bass with a number of good jazz groups in Amsterdam. Then, later, we had seen each other when he turned up on the jazz scene in Paris. In fact it turned out that both of us had become friends with Django Reinhardt — quite independently of each other, but at more or less the same time. Jaap had come to England by sea, arriving at the coast of England with his father and brother. It was hard to believe that the three of them came all this way in a rowing boat, against the odds of weather and tide and fog and possible detection, odds which must have been staggering. They rowed hour after hour, blinded by the mists and the heavy clouds overhead, so that they might well have been rowing tragically in to the endless open seas of the North Atlantic. But Jaap, in a very brave way, simply said, 'We had to leave!'

The last news I had had of Jaap had been at the very start of the war when he had left France and returned to Holland. There had been a story that he might have been sent off to one of the German camps. Now it turned out that Jaap had come to see me with some of the best news I had had for two years. It was about my parents: he had seen them only days before he left Holland. It was very strange how it came about.

Shortly after I had arrived in England as a refugee, *Melody Maker*, a music magazine with a large circulation, had run a long story about me and my music, and about my escape from Europe. It had included a photograph showing a large picture of me propped on the corner of the desk belonging to Pat Brand, editor of *Melody Maker*. Some time later that great American jazz magazine *Downbeat* had picked up the story in New York and had run it in full, complete with the picture.

Since America and Germany were not at war in 1940 or 1941, the Germans allowed some American publications into Germany and the occupied countries. Somehow, a copy of that issue of *Downbeat* had appeared in Holland, and the usually meticulous German censors had missed the story of a Dutchman's escape from the Nazis. Jaap had seen it. He didn't live very far from my parents in Amsterdam so he went over that same day to see them.

The last time I had seen or heard of my parents was just before the war in 1939, more than two years earlier. They had no way of telling where I was or whether I was alive or dead. Jaap told me they insisted that he read the article to them over and over, and how ecstatic my mother and father were to learn I was safe.

As for my parents, they were not only alive, but so far

they had survived fairly decently. Jaap told me that my father had been forced to work about twelve hours a day, six days a week in a forced-labour camp, but at least had the privilege of being able to go home for Saturday and Sunday nights. It gave me great hope that perhaps my premonitions were wrong. I told myself to forget thinking that the worst was going to happen. I was just being too anxious! But then who wouldn't be, after hearing all the horror stories about life under Nazi Germany? That was the last news I was to hear about them until Holland was free.

By 1942 I had been in the Army for well over a year. Jimmy Kirk and I had begun by playing music for ourselves, and Jimmy had even joined the camp band, but then we had decided it was time to form our own group. Eventually we made up a small jazz combo of bass, drums, piano, accordion, a singer and harmonica.

There was one hitch: in the entire camp there wasn't a drummer worth his sticks. So during this time I taught myself to play drums and found myself doing what musicians call 'doubling' — playing harmonica and drums. We began to play at the officers' dances, on holidays and for small concerts on the base. Pretty soon we were playing at almost every camp within fifty miles. This brought us a lot of perks, because we quickly became popular and were asked by the English services to play at their camps. But I still found myself needing to escape completely from the camp atmosphere, and I started going to London with every pass I had. It was a long way, and expensive, so I decided to try and get a little work from the BBC while I was in London, to pay for these trips. I got work so regularly that it surprised me. All I had to do was ask Radio Variety and they seemed to find a booking. Part of the reason was that jazz had been around a very short time in England, and so it was a young man's game — but most of the young were in the services so there was a shortage of players. Then there was the fact that I was a foreign ally, and therefore good for the cause. And the final fact was that I was very popular with the people at the BBC. As a result, Max Geldray's harmonica was on the radio often, and I became fairly well known in wartime Britain.

It was two o'clock on Thursday morning when I received an order to proceed immediately to see the Brigade Commander. When you are in the Army a summons to the Commander's office is one thing but a summons to see the Commander himself is another! It can never mean anything good, whether you are guilty or innocent! So on the walk across to his office I had visions which ranged all the way from extra duty to a firing squad. My friend Ben de Koning, the pianist of our band, had also been summoned.

'You are going to get a new uniform, and it will be a good one! You are dismissed.' The Brigade Commander did not smile, so it wasn't a joke. But I kept thinking to myself, is this the Dutch equivalent of a hearty meal? That the condemned man should look nice?

It was three weeks later that we were finally told what we were going to do — although, for security reasons, not where we were going to do it. It seemed we were to be part of the entertainment for a royal birthday: that of Princess Elizabeth, who would be sixteen on 21 April. I was to play the harmonica, and Ben would be my accompanist.

We were driven to London and deposited among a group of people who were obviously musicians and entertainers — and off we went in convoy, in tight security, to Windsor Castle.

I suppose that the castle has since been visited by a hundred million tourists, but at that time not many people had seen inside that marvellous building. In wartime England all the valuable paintings and works of art, and the more precious of the rugs and furniture, had been removed. The chandeliers burned brightly, but the windows were covered over in compliance with blackout regulations and the place was almost bare of furniture so the castle was very stark inside. The only furnishings in the room we were taken to were great long tables covered with white tablecloths. But in keeping with the Royal Family's promise to ration themselves as the public was, there was no great banquet spread. Instead, there were hundreds of goblets in a line,

bowls of non-alcoholic fruit punch, and crystal decanters
filled with drink from the royal cellars.

I felt both overwhelmed and underdressed for this
assemblage. For a start, there seemed to be no military
people here below the rank of colonel, and the stylish and
highly decorated dress uniforms made it look as though we
were about to begin a military ball. Judging by the number
of medals people were wearing, everyone seemed to have
fought in every battle since Balaclava. We stood there —
plain, unheralded and most un-English — balancing from
foot to foot.

After a few moments I noticed one of the butlers gazing
at us from the other side of the long table. He smiled slightly,
and then leaned forward and said, 'Perhaps a Scotch whisky,
sir? From the King's cellar!'

I am certain he felt sympathy for these poor lost foreign
foot-soldiers, and so he decided to bring a smile (or at least
a silly grin) to our faces. Whatever the reason, he poured us
very stiff drinks of this elixir, and we proceeded to let it glide
gently down our throats. I am told that just as the present
queen knows her horseflesh, so the late king knew his
Scotch whisky. It was undoubtedly three times as old as I
was, and marvellously smooth and tasty to boot. It was also
potent!

When my barman smiled again and asked if I would like
a refill, I shook my head and gave him the silly grin he had
been waiting for. The whisky was still marvellously smooth.
And still potent. By the time that His Majesty and Her
Majesty entered the room with their daughters, I was so
anaesthetized that I found myself stamping my feet to be
sure they were still there.

But an hour later, when we entered the theatre in the castle,
I was stone-cold sober — and so was everyone else in our
party. I suppose that is what royal performances do to you!

It was a lovely little theatre, holding perhaps three
hundred people. In the front row sat King George VI and
Queen Elizabeth with the two princesses. But the
atmosphere wasn't stiff and 'royal' in any sense, it was like
a family gathering — filled with fun and laughter and honest

joy. I suppose it had to do with being in one of their own homes, and being in this personal gathering. But there was none of that sense of royal decorum you might find in most public settings. It was, after all, the sixteenth birthday of Princess Elizabeth — and she was obviously someone much loved by her parents.

At the reception afterwards the lady who is now the Queen Mother did most of the talking for the family. Her husband, the King, seemed to stay in the background, which made him seem a very gentle and almost shy man. I can see the way this family has garnered loyalty among the people who surround them. There *is* something special about them.

Shortly after that night in Windsor Castle I was sent a gramophone album of recordings made on that stage. It was signed by each of the members of the Royal Family. It is a precious possession to this day.

7

Battlegrounds

ALTHOUGH I WAS in the Princess Irene Brigade for five years, my experience in battle was short and very limited. It is not a hero's story, but it is a soldier's story. And it is a fact that what happened during that brief time did alter the course of my life.

Although I have told you that much of my time in the Army was spent giving concerts and playing for dances, there was also the serious business of training to be a soldier. It was the Army's version of aerobic fitness exercises: slogging along in full kit in the heavy rain, running up and down hills until we could run great distances without breathing hard, learning to crawl silently and, or course, learning to shoot. Rather like Jane Fonda in Army boots.

But the fact is that the difference between training for war, and the real thing, is like writing about war as opposed to living through it. We were still stationed near Wolverhampton in the Midlands, and for months the rumours had been persistent that any day now we would be going off to land somewhere on the coast of France. Several dozen times, generally in the middle of the night, we would be hauled out of bed and put through the practice of shipping out. We would load ourselves with all our gear, climbing into the trucks, and drive off for a short trip to nowhere.

On this occasion it was some time in the earlier part of the evening, that we received the order to pack up our gear and get ready to load. It was a very dark night, and very cool too. In fact it was really one of the more pleasant nights to go through a practice.

But I believe that, somehow, almost everyone sensed that

we were in for something more than practice. Perhaps it was because the officers seemed more serious about the whole business, or perhaps they seemed a little more nervous. Whatever it was, we knew. I heard one of my pals ask, 'This is it?' And someone answered simply 'Right!'

Beside the trucks were three mountains of supplies that you had to add to your regular duffle: a load of food; a kit they called 'survival'; and of course, a supply of ammunition.

In some way I suppose that each of us in those trucks felt like crusaders off to liberate our land. There was a great deal of chat among all of us, but then, after we had been on the road a while, it quietened down and for long stretches no one said a word. I noticed my hands had begun to shake slightly and my feet, which had been perspiring, now felt icy cold. I was feeling the effects of a great surge of adrenalin. And the first symptoms of raw nerves.

The gear was bulky and my clothes were thick and coarse, and everything felt very heavy. The convoy had picked up a great deal of speed, and now the back of that truck was infernally noisy. I did the best thing you can do when you are under that kind of stress: I fell asleep and didn't wake up until we were near the docks of London.

There was an air raid over the City as we arrived, and while it wasn't over our part of the waterfront, it made us very nervous. We knew we weren't headed for any kind of shelter, and that we were exactly what the *Luftwaffe* was looking for.

We were broken into several groups and loaded aboard Liberty ships. We found ourselves put into the hold, as though we were being stored. We were told to crawl into the hammocks that had been put up, and stay there, so that we wouldn't roll and fall over each other when we got to sea. Our quarters were filled with the heavy smell of bunker oil and men. It was a long time before the ship began to move, but when it did get started there was a little breeze of fresh, cool air below deck, and we felt less stifled. Then there was a lot of talk and joking and, although there was hardly any light in the place, someone shouted, 'Who's brought the cards?' The hold filled with manic laughter, as though this were the best joke of the week. Once again I fell asleep in total exhaustion.

Hours and hours later, when our landing craft bounced on to the beach, there seemed to be men, tanks, trucks, guns and piles of supplies everywhere — lying there exposed as though the enemy was far away. But we knew they were right there. We could hear their guns, as well as our own guns from the ships and those on the shoreline far down the beach on our right, where the Canadians and the British were landing. Then waves of our planes began to pass overhead, and we heard the thump, thump, thump of hundreds of bombs exploding ahead. Welcome to Normandy!

I felt like an observer. I know that I took in all these sights in a matter of seconds, but they seemed to stretch into a very long time. Then we started to move, and I experienced that feeling you have when you wake from a heavy sleep after a vivid dream — still half asleep and not sure which world is real.

We ran across the beach and up an embankment, between the narrow lines of a yellow rope that the Corps of Engineers had strung up like a roadway between a field of mines. There must have been fifty of us in our group, all of us staggering in the sand from the weight of our packs. We double-timed it across the sand and up a bank, and then we began to crawl toward a long hedge fifty feet in front of us. Under the cover of the hedge an officer stopped us and pointed to a slight rise of high ground ahead of us. It was high ground surrounded by trees, and he told us we were to head for those woods. But to get there we would have to cross about a hundred yards of open ground — and the Germans were in the woods.

In ones and twos we ran across that open space. Because of the noise and confusion of the artillery and the bombs, we couldn't tell whether or not the Germans were firing at us. But the chances are they were. Several of the men who had gone ahead had dropped their kits as they ran, and when my turn came I understood why. It had rained for several days previously and the ground was soft and spongy, as well as being very uneven. As I ran forward, that immense pack started swaying back and forth behind me. It was knocking me off balance so much that I had visions of falling down and, like a turtle on its back, never being able to get up again.

I slipped off the straps and dropped everything but the ammunition. I might let myself starve to death, but I wouldn't die undefended. After that, while I didn't run at Olympic speeds, I certainly did set personal-best records.

As we ran across that field we had to avoid small trenches in the ground. It looked as though someone had stopped to dig depressions — depressions which ran for yards and yards, parallel to the way we were running. Then I saw the wreck of a glider and I realized this was where the airborne assault troops had landed to push the Germans off our beach. When we got into the woods it was another time to bless them, for they had come in and built foxholes and dug-outs, all ready made for us to move in. When it was that the Airborne had been in and slipped away I do not know, I do know they must have been hellishly good fighters. And astonishingly brave men.

Our orders were simply to hold the line. The British and the Canadians were on one side and the Americans on the other. Their job was to advance and form a pincer movement — which, ironically, is a German term for a tactic which means to surround and enclose. We didn't have to move anywhere! And I have to admit that I was happy about that.

It is now a long time since that war, so I won't assume that you know much about foxholes and dug-outs. A foxhole is a roundish hole dug about five feet down into the ground. It is wide enough for a soldier and his gear and not so deep that he can't, with great effort, pull himself out of it. If we could have made our burrows ten feet deep and still get out, believe me we would have.

Because soldiers want to have something ready and handy to jump into wherever they happen to be, a number of foxholes are dug around a campsite,

But our main digs (if you will pardon the atrocious pun) were in the form of dug-outs. This was where we lived and

where we watched. Picture it as a kind of earthen pillbox.
They were dug into the side, or near the top, of a hillside;
at the front there was an observation opening with a few
sandbags packed around it. You got into the thing by way
of a crawl trench roofed with tree trunks and branches. A
dug-out became a home for two, looking out toward the
German lines.

The entire time I sat in that observation post I never saw
a German. And although intermittently I would fire toward
their lines, as we were supposed to do, I don't think I ever
hit anyone. I don't regret that! But even if I couldn't see
them and I couldn't shoot them, I could sometimes hear
them.

I was surprised by the fact that war, that noisiest of man's
endeavours, could have its quiet times. For an hour or so,
one side or the other would lay down a deafening barrage
of fire, and then it would be deathly still. When your ears
stopped ringing and we could hear again, it was as though
we were living in a second world.

We could hear the clanging of German mess gear and hear
them shouting to each other. When the wind was right we
could hear the voices plainly, though I could never make out
the words themselves. And one night I even heard someone
sing, although I am not sure what the tune was or where it
came from. During these quiet times when there was no
firing, the two of us in the dug-out would chain-smoke
cigarettes and talk non-stop, as though we had to get in all
the talking we could before they started up again.

During those first few days in France, German artillery
had been aimed at the emplacements on the beach and at the
ships behind us. Allied artillery seemed to be aimed at the
big German guns far ahead of us, and the planes, which
came swooping over our heads and skimmed the trees,
would fire their guns well ahead of us too. It felt as though
we were stationed between the battles. But then that all
changed.

The Germans now began shooting directly at our lines
with artillery, grenades, mortars and bullets. We launched
the same attack, although neither side moved an inch. Most

of the time we spent underground, hoping that the next bang to hit the ground and shake our cave could not be closer.

We had been at the front a week and, while I have never thought of myself as a particularly brave man, I think somehow I was getting used to this life. I found myself numbed at times, curled up and uncomfortable, but still able to sleep no matter what. When I was awake I was continually alert and ready. Tuned-in — to react and survive.

If it is possible to be comfortable in war, the Princess Irene Brigade was comfortable at that moment. There had been an unusually long lull in the action on our part of the front, and it didn't take long to feel the security of that. But then an officer came up to our dug-out and told us we should stand ready. We were probably going to move forward some time that day.

Under those circumstances we came to expect that one of two things would happen. The first scenario had the Germans retreating, and our troops marching in for the chase. The other scenario had the artillery laying down a barrage, the Air Force following in and carpet-bombing the place, and then foot soldiers advancing into the inferno. Well, it didn't happen either way!

Hours and hours passed. We could hear the occasional pop of gunfire on our left and right, but no barrage or sounds of aircraft that night.

But what a strange relief it was, our senses were heightened with the adrenalin of the day, and our feelings were hard to understand. I kept wishing that, whatever the cost, we could get on with it. I swear I could hear the Germans talking more loudly that night than I had ever heard them before. Perhaps they too felt that something was in the wind.

Just after daylight I decided to leave the dug-out for a few moments, to have a fast wash and get some food. One minute I was standing in the sun, with my mess tin in my hand, the next there were smashing explosions all around me.

Everyone not already underground was running for cover, and I remember that instinctively I found the first foxhole and dived into it head first. I must have been about half-way into the hole when I felt as though I had been snapped in two. I remember feeling the trunk of my body twist and then slap the bottom of the foxhole, as my legs were whipped forward by the concussion, and my knees crashed into the lip of the hole. The next memory I had after that was of lying on one shoulder and on one cheek, with my head twisted and my feet still pointing up in the air.

I don't remember pain, or even the relief of being alive. I just felt detached. My body was doubled over into a position which should have been excruciating, but I just lay there. I don't know how long I was there, and I couldn't even remember why I was there until, with one eye, I peered up and saw a face peering down at me. I heard the voice say, in Dutch, 'For God's sake. This is not a time to sleep!'

Several years ago a friend asked me about this story and wanted to know what I did next. I told him that, although I didn't know where I was or where I was going, I simply got out of that foxhole and started to run. But, in fact, I am sure I must have moved more like a staggering drunk. And, although I had no idea what I was doing, some instinct took me to the large First Aid dug-out. I got to the entrance and collapsed.

This dug-out was just behind our lines; here the dead were gathered, and others were patched up, just enough to get them to the hospital behind the lines. Over the next thirty-six hours I stayed at this First Aid post: awake some of the time and unconscious most of the time. As in all hospitals, I can remember that at one stage they woke me to give me medicine: pills known as 'blockbusters' because they knocked the patients out for hours at a time. Then, some time in that second or third day, I was loaded into an ambulance and sent back behind the lines.

Later on, I asked why I was held so long at that dressing station at the front. The answers I got ranged from: 'We thought we might get you back in the line . . .' 'There was no transport' to: 'There was no room at the hospital.' About two months later I met the doctor who had treated me at the front. He was at the same hospital as I was, with a badly broken leg. He gave me a fourth reason: 'We thought you were going to die.'

The hospital behind the lines was really a series of very large tents. It was rough and ready, like something from the television series 'M*A*S*H,' but a lot better than the dug-outs at the front. I seemed to be in a ward reserved for people in shock. There were very few wounded, and even those who were wounded seemed to have very superficial injuries. But there were lots of other symptoms.

All around me were people who couldn't walk or stand. Men who shook continuously and uncontrollably. Those who screamed or wept, whether awake or dreaming. Several became violent. But the most common symptom among all those soldiers was that they could not talk. And this silence, and the way they stared out at the world, was the most frightening symptom of all. It is a part of war we seldom hear about, and yet it is as devastating as bombs.

My own symptoms were less dramatic. I had recurring nightmares which left me wet and shaking, and feeling that somehow my body had been compressed and squeezed to become something with the weight of lead. But after that first week I began to improve — at least enough to travel. And I found myself shipped off home ... back to England.

In England the hospital was again made up of tents, but it was in the flower-filled grounds of a peaceful country estate. In this setting it was hard to believe there had ever been a war, and it helped immeasurably in putting minds back together. But still I could not look people in the eye, and I would continuously stare at the ground as I walked about. If I tried to look up, and gazed around me, my eyes would immediately fall back to the ground and, often, I would begin to cry.

I was in that hospital for several months. Hospital days are not something most of us want to dwell on. And my recollections of that time are not too vivid anyway — our brains have a habit of editing out much of our memory when it is full of disagreeable pain and sadness. But there is one occasion I do remember very vividly. I was in a large room, sitting in front of a panel of doctors. The head man was a psychiatrist, and he did most of the talking.

'We think that your bad times are pretty well over Max,' he said. 'We are going to send you back to your camp, but I think that your fighting days are over.'

Another doctor remarked on their surprise at how well I had come out of this physically — maybe that I was alive at all! The concussion had been enormous and yet, although I was short and slight, I had come through it all much more rapidly than the hefty six-footers who were all over the hospital.

'We were surprised there was no collapse or extensive damage to your lungs.' he said. 'What is it you do for a living?' When I told him he said, 'Ah, ha!' and I was allowed to leave.

I don't mean to stretch the point. And I do know that I could have been a tuba player, a glass blower, or a man with a deaf wife, and I might have had the same lung power. But I was a harmonica player, and because of that I had enlarged the capacity of my lungs and the strength of the controlling muscles. The harmonica, if it hadn't saved my life, certainly helped get me back in one piece. Three days later I was back at camp in Wolverhampton.

Three months after the invasion of Normandy, on 4 September 1944, Brussels was liberated. I travelled to Brussels several times while the war in Europe still raged. Because I was on inactive duty I had the time, so I hitched a ride on a transport from a nearby Air Force base. I was literally stuffed into the back of a Dakota transport, and rubbed shoulders with a power generator the size of a small house. It is hard to explain why I wanted to go there. Brussels had always been one of my favourite cities, that is true, and I did — and do — know many people there. But it had something to do with being closer to the war.

One of the things I've tried to explain to myself, in the years since those times, is the strange feeling I had about the war. When you are at a battle front, if you aren't afraid, then the next thing that can be said about you is that you are crazy. It seemed that every other minute I was dreaming about the day when it would all just go away. I began to understand why people hope for a small wound, so that they can get out of it alive. But then, when it happened to me, when I got away from the battle, I had a strong sense of emptiness — as though the job was unfinished.

Psychologists have tried to explain this by saying that a sudden normal life is an anti-climax, that it lacks that edge of danger and drama. They say that there is the guilt of getting through alive. They base it on the fact that there is a special camaraderie of spirit which people find in a war. They even say it's like a withdrawal from the drug of fear. I have no idea whether any of that is true. I do know that, almost inconceivably, I wanted to go back!

There is almost a little shame in this statement, but my feelings of wanting to go back to the war were not about being a champion of the free world, or beating down the Nazi horde. And I wasn't feeling a need for revenge or bravery. The feelings had nothing to do with being a war junkie; either; my Army experience wasn't the kind I wanted to sit and reminisce about with pals, as though those had been the best times. The truth is I just wanted to beat those other guys — I just wanted to help end it. And at that point, if I had been in danger, and close to losing my life, I am not sure it would have mattered that much to me. I have talked to a number of veterans about their feelings and often I have heard them tell me of a similar feeling. It may be where bravery, or lunacy, comes from.

Planes seemed to be taking off or landing every minute of the day when I made that first trip back to Brussels. I was surprised at how little it had changed physically, although the hustle of war made it seem much more vibrant than I had remembered it. If I thought it was going to get me closer to the war, though, I was quite wrong. The war was less than a hundred miles away in the north, and yet it could have been a thousand. I went back and forth to Brussels about six times, as though I was going to a launching-area for my return to Amsterdam. But the launching was to wait many months.

Holland was almost the last occupied country to be a battlefield during the Second World War. Brussels was

liberated in September, around the same time that Holland
was invaded by the Allies at Arnhem, but it wasn't until the
following May, eight months to the day, that the Germans
surrendered. Actually they surrendered in Holland on the
fourth of May, just three days before their total surrender in
Germany on the seventh. So I didn't get to Holland until the
latter part of May. Those months had been an agonizing
period for me, being so close to Holland and yet unable to
get there. Then Amsterdam was liberated and I found myself
on my way to the very street on which my family had lived.
I remember asking myself, 'Why am I doing this?'

I expected many signs of war when I arrived in
Amsterdam, but the city looked very much the same. There
was no rubble in the streets, no signs of devastation, and
very few bullet-pocked walls. If it looked dreary, it had to
do with the lack of flowers in a city I'd always known as
being alive with them. If it seemed run down, I felt that some
paint and a little sprucing up would do the job. The people
were another matter. I had never thought of it before, but of
course the Dutch, like people all over Europe, were going
to have to learn to live a normal life again. Learn to live with
freedom. In the aftermath of all the joy and exhilaration at
being free, I thought I could now feel their sense of
uncertainty. People on the street would nod and wave and
smile when they saw the Dutch insignia on my uniform, and
one man even slapped my arm in pride, but they had very
few words to say to me.

The shadow of those years of occupation stayed for a long
time in Holland.

I was standing in front of the building where my parents
had lived, finding it hard to take those next few steps. A
small boy on a battered tricycle came up to me and asked in
English, 'Are you Canadian? Do you have any candy?'
When I answered in Dutch, he seemed surprised that anyone
in uniform could speak his language.

Inside the building I met a number of our neighbours, and
I asked them what they knew, or had heard. The answers
gave me very little news about my parents, but told me a
great deal about life under Hitler. The German plan had been

to make certain that the country knew the consequences and the terror of putting up a resistance. So when they invaded Holland, they did it with all the violence they could muster. From the air they levelled much of Rotterdam as an object lesson.

But once resistance had gone, and they had moved in as conquerors, they set out to assure the people that, so long as everyone behaved, there would be no consequences. They assured the Dutch that they were very civilized, and that the war horror stories were Churchill's propaganda. They treated everyone rather courteously at first. As a small first action, they began to segregate the Jewish children into special schools. Then they designed special restrictions for certain Dutch Protestants, Catholics and Jews. Then all the Jews were to be segregated. But still, they were not yet too harsh an occupier. Then they required that all Jews wear the Star of David — and public blame and ridicule was increased. And then it became unsafe to be in the wrong place at the wrong time. The trouble was, no one knew what the wrong place or the wrong time was.

My father was sent to work and live at a nearby labour camp. Although the labour was exhausting, and he had lost weight and developed a cough, he had remained safe. Over those years he had even been able to come home on the weekends, arriving late on Saturday night and returning to the camp on Sunday. One weekend, in 1944, he had simply not come home. There was no way of finding out about him. At that time an enquirer might have been shot for asking.

The neighbours told me that, after the first shock, my mother had been calm and reconciled. The German military were known to sell off the possessions of people they seized; they used the money for their war chest or themselves. So my mother began giving away almost all her valuable possessions to her neighbours and her friends. She and my sister lived in the bare flat for several months after that. Several non-Jewish friends had offered to take my sister and hide her from the Germans, but my sister had refused to leave my mother. Perhaps it was a comfort to them both, that when they were taken they were taken together.

I have told you that my mother gave away everything of value. That is true, except for the one thing she left behind for me. It is strange, the faith she had that I would survive the war, come back to Amsterdam and then, unbelievably, find the neighbour with whom she had left a special gift.

The König family lived in rooms behind the little grocery store which they had run since I was a boy. It was about five doorways down from the entranceway to our building. All the Königs had survived the war: the father, the mother, and twin daughters who were now about fifteen. We sat in the kitchen talking very quietly, and then, after an hour or so, Mr König left the room to get a trunk that my mother had left for me. It wasn't a large trunk, more the size we used in the Army as foot lockers at the end of our bed. It was stuffed full of personal things my mother had made for our home: special things like embroidered cloths and sheets and hand-made spreads. And there were pieces of jewellery. Not valuable jewellery, but pieces I had seen her wear on special occasions and at family gatherings. But the most valuable things in the trunk were the albums of photographs.

I had never seen most of these before, and those I had seen had always been scattered about our home in shoe-boxes and drawers. Now they were neatly arranged in small photo albums: tiny pictures, dimmed by time, each labelled with who and where and when. The photographs spanned the years from long before I was born, until the last time we were all together. And even a few pictures from the years after that. They remain one of the great treasures of my life.

8

The Coming of the Goons

I WAS DEMOBBED from The Princess Irene Brigade in 1945, and I decided I would go back to Brussels. I suppose I hoped that the city would be lucky for me once again, but in fact there was very little sense of the old Brussels left. The sense of joy seemed to have gone out of the place, and the clubs were either filled with roistering drunks or were settings for quiet, almost solemn, drinkers. And music didn't seem to fit into either scene. So for weeks I sat around and promised that tomorrow I would seriously go about the business of finding work.

I had been there for about a month, and was on the verge of leaving the music business and taking a job, any job to make survival money, when out of the blue I had a letter from my old boss in Paris, Ray Ventura. I have often wondered what kind of crystal ball he must have had to find out that I was still alive and living in Belgium. I packed my gear and took the next train to Paris.

I spent the next two years working with the Ventura Orchestra in Paris. Going back to my old, familiar world was a marvellous way of getting back into the civilian world again. But times had changed: the radio shows were gone and the touring was drying up. The French public did not seem to be interested in things that reminded them of times before the war. In 1947 the Ray Ventura Orchestra was dis-banded — an apt word if ever there was one. A piece of French musical history was over.

I was thirty-one, and was about to start another stage of my musical career. I returned to England.

By 1949 I had been in England about twenty months: Harry

S. Truman was beginning a second term as president in the
US; the Berlin blockade was lifted by the Russians;
Hungarian Communists were purging thousands; the North
Atlantic Pact was signed; and just a few months earlier
Wilhelmina of the Netherlands had abdicated in favour of
Juliana. Many momentous things were happening in the
world. There were even strong feelings about bigger and
better times — but I didn't seem to be included in them.

If I thought I had been through lean financial times before,
I really hit the next level in London. I was working regularly,
but my pay was so low I could hardly pack in enough work
to pay the rent. It is hard to believe, but there was I, working
in the glamour field of clubs and BBC Radio, receiving fan
mail and sometimes being recognized on the street, yet I
earned little more than the average cab driver. And I had to
have a wardrobe!

I needed a break.

I had met a great many people at the BBC, and one of them
turned out to be a fan. His name was Patrick Dixon, and he
was a radio producer who loved jazz. He would telephone me
quite regularly, and ask me to come to his office to listen to
a new recording. Then we would sit there and talk about
music for the next few hours.

On one of those occasions, as we sat talking about jazz and
about my own playing, Pat began talking about my performance
on a recent show, and he went on to praise me lavishly.

As much as I enjoyed the music, and being in Pat's
company, I could not let that cue go by. I said, 'Pat, I really
appreciate what you have to say about my playing, but I wish
some time you would give me a broadcast!'

Pat looked at me for a long moment, then said, 'Yes, that's
true, isn't it? I've never had you on one of my programmes. But
I will, Max. Just you wait. I'll find the right one for you!'

Pat Dixon was true to his word. One day he telephoned me
and told me he was producing a 'trial recording' — the BBC's
term for a pilot show. The following Sunday afternoon they
were going to record that show, 'Crazy People', and he said
he thought this was the show for me that he'd been waiting
for. I suppose he was right. Two years later it had grown into

a series, and was renamed. It was now 'The Goon Show'.

I shall always be grateful to Pat: a man of talent, dedication, spirit and great generosity. It is a sad fact that the entertainment business has too few Pat Dixons. Fortunately there are a few. But, as my dear friend Michael Bentine always says, 'A bloody, bloody few!'

'The Goon Show revolutionized radio comedy,' states a respected biographical dictionary. The four comedians — Spike Milligan, Peter Sellers, Harry Secombe and Michael Bentine (who left after July 1952) — first performed together on radio in May 1951 in a programme billed as 'Crazy People, featuring radio's own Crazy Gang —"The Goons" '. About eighteen months later the programme was gaining fans all over the country and, at Spike's insistence, the programme was officially re-christened 'The Goon Show' in November 1952. Over the years Milligan wrote most of the scripts and played (among others), Eccles the utterly irresponsible idiot, Minnie Bannister and Count Jim Moriarty; Peter Sellers used his brilliance at mimicry to play a host of bizarre characters, including Henry Crun, Hercules Grytpype-Thynne, Major Dennis Bloodnok and Bluebottle, while Harry Secombe's main role was that of Neddie Seagoon, the central character in most of the shows who was constantly embarking on heroically stupid missions.

The Goon Show did more than revolutionize radio comedy; it revolutionized my life as well. The programmes were all pre-recorded on the Sunday before transmission, and I — with my harmonica — was there. I took part in all the shows: in *The Goon Show Companion* (published by Robson Books) Roger Wilmut writes : 'The musicians contribute more than melody to the show. Geldray, possibly the world's worst actor, takes a few odd lines . . .'!

As part of the Goons I have been asked a thousand times about Peter and Harry and Spike. But I have always been wary of those 'what was he like' questions, and the very narrow truths they produce. So for a long time, instead of trying to deal with the question, I would answer with a stock set of short anecdotal stories. The stories I told were meant to confirm that the Goons were simply entertainingly odd-ball characters. They always seemed to satisfy people's curiosity quickly.

Of course the Goon fanatics were a little different. They didn't seem to care for entertaining answers to their questions: what they wanted instead was affirmation of what they believed. And invariably these Goonophiles zeroed in on Milligan.

They would say things like: Don't you think Milligan was the most creative? Or the most eccentric, or the most volatile, or the most crazy. Spike always seemed to be 'the most' something. But the fact is that he is not a convenient entity, and he was always far too complicated and original a personality to be described by a list of adjectives.

I always tend to think of Spike's character visually. I remember seeing him in an English costume drama many years ago, playing the part of a Court Herald. He had on a coarse and bulky cloak, together with a hat which resembled an overstuffed pot-holder, and short trunks which were joined at the bottom by an appropriately risqué exposure of fashionable hose. To understate the matter, his was neither an imposing figure, nor a dandy one.

There was a very long and elegant scene in the midst of a crowded imperial court. Our hero stood there shouting something which sounded like heraldic madness. None of the people at court seemed to be listening, so he got louder. Eventually a royal person nodded slightly, and the guards grabbed the herald and carted him off to the dungeons. (As the plot later revealed, this was a mistake; while half of the message had concerned itself with the price of goat meat, the other half was about an enemy army two miles away.)

Why do I associate this scene of Spike the actor, with Spike the man? It's because of the parallels! First, Spike could drive you nuts while he was trying to save your life! Second, those dark and ancient days fitted him as a background much better than anything in the twentieth century does.

Born in 1918 in India to an Irish father in the British Army, even to this day Spike seems to me to retain some of the sound and flavour of Poona and Rangoon. I sense it sometimes in

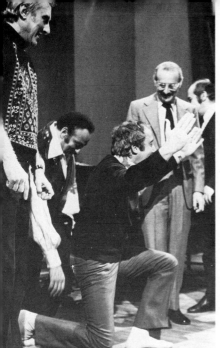

It was impossible to keep a
straight face – even on stage!

The original 'Goon With the Wind'!

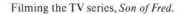
Filming the TV series, *Son of Fred*.

Max and Peter Sellers in Hollywood.

Max in a TV pilot show for NBC in Hollywood.   Recording in Hollywood.

Max's wife Susan,
son Philip (a rock drummer) and Max.

Max's 70th birthday party. Family
members gathered around him
include his wife, Susan, son Philip,
daughters Holly and Judy, daughter-
in-law Chue and son-in-law Roger.
Max's old friend Michael Bentine
can be seen at the back of the group.

Max and 'The Blow Hards' at the Stroke Center in Palm Springs.

Former President Gerald Ford, Mrs Betty Ford and Max. A picture taken at the annual 'Jazz Without Booze' concert where Max has appeared for the past five years. Rancho Mirage, California, February 1989.

the sharp clipped way he speaks. At other times, almost in the way he thinks. Certainly, often, in the way he writes.

I think the time Spike spent serving in the Second World War, and his memory of his father's unhappy experiences with the Army (he was unexpectedly discharged when Spike was about eleven, leading to financial hardship for the Milligans, and to Spike — not yet in his teens — having to take on dull manual jobs to help support the family) had a great deal to do with the fact that, throughout all the years of the Goon Show, there was a recurring theme that 'took the mickey' out of the military, an officer class he depicted as possessing unlimted degrees of pompous incompetence. One has only think of Major Dennis Bloodnok, Ind. Arm. Rtd. (Military idiot, coward and bar).

The Goons inevitably met people from all classes, including the highest. Harry Secombe could always make himself comfortable in the company of the titled, right up to the level of royalty. Peter, although he was a good friend of Princess Margaret and Anthony Armstrong-Jones, was always much less comfortable with other royal presences. Of course we had all known Tony, the Earl of Snowdon, since his days as a photographer; he had done many of the publicity sessions with the Goons when we did television shows, like 'A Show Called Fred' and the 'Son of Fred' series in 1956. But Spike much preferred the company of his own pals, whether writers, or just the kind of ordinary people who run his favourite fish and chip shop.

For ten years, and well over two hundred programmes, Spike Milligan was the central force of the Goon Show. He was the one who forced the BBC into new directions. While there was always a producer on the show, it was Spike who was the manic and inventive driving force behind every detail of the production. I don't wish to take anything away from the brilliant writers who from time to time worked with Spike: Larry Stephens, Jimmy Grafton, Eric Sykes, or any of the others who contributed lines, ideas and whole segments to the programme, but Spike was the special catalyst. And, in this case, that had a very special meaning. Week in and week out, Spike was the central figure in putting all that comedy writing together, 'the tool which fitted and held it all together' as a reviewer once wrote, suggesting that he was the spanner which tightened the nuts and bolts of the other Goons' talent.

But if Spike held it all together, he could also be one of the most annoying people you could meet. (I once described our relationship as a love-sock relationship!) For the Goon Show, this meant almost continuous raucous rounds with the BBC brass.

Sometime in the early 1950s Michael Bentine described the BBC brass as 'a moribund collection of interfering knighthood aspirants'. That is not to say that they were a group you would characterize as being seriously bad. But they were practitioners of misplaced propriety, and they suffered from terminally dulled sensitivities in every other regard, too!

Into this unadmirable collection stepped Spike Milligan, and appearing with all the panache of a walking unmade bed. A jerk-gaited individualist with a rude tongue. A man whose very smile suggested irreparable calamity. He and they did not mix well.

The impresarios of BBC Broadcast Rules had a no-no list which, though unpublished, seemed to extend over a very broad area. It held that references to the religious, political or military sphere, or to that of the ruling class, were not acceptable in a vehicle such as the Goon Show. In addition, the merest satirical mention of the Royals was tantamount to treason. This, even though it was widely known that the Royal Family were great fans of the show. By today's standards, the shows were pretty tame — gentle lampooning, with the odd double entendre and naughtiness thrown in. But that was an age in which some considered even the word 'poop' inappropriate for English ears.

Through the war years, and those following them, this conservatism had cut down on all kinds of creativity at the BBC — and the results were to be heard on the air. There was some fine talent and some very entertaining programmes, but for the most part BBC Radio had a philosophy (philosophy and policy being totally interchangeable words) of 'responsible programming'. It might be argued that comedy programming was prospering, because there was a lot of it and it was suitably decorous and good-naturedly funny.

But Spike was never quite satisfied with that approach to radio broadcasting. He insisted on bringing a wild (if not very imposing) grandeur to mother BBC. But mostly what he brought was innovation!

Later on, this was to become a disturbing dilemma for the upper BBC echelons. They coveted the Goon Show's success, but they hated the unbridled Milligan — and, of course, the necessity of doing his programmes.

I think that, to a man, the Goons and their producers appreciated that Spike bore the brunt of the attack. It was quite a brunt! Arguing over humour! And all that shouting, cajoling, pouting, convincing, brooding, hostility and worry took its toll of Spike. Some of it may still be there, like the unresolved hurt many of us bury inside ourselves. But before your sympathies rise to too high a level, let me tell you that he was a cunning devil too. He would use his reputation as an eccentric to beat down the opposition and confuse them. And I remember that Peter Sellers used to say that Spike had a special gift for explaining simple things so that you could not understand them.

Freud suggested that you could find the man through his dreams. I once heard a second-hand account of a dream that Spike had! It began with cardiologist Spike Milligan doing assembly-line heart surgery on a group of BBC Heads of Programming. But, no matter how deep he cut, or how much rummaging he did, he could never find that particular organ. After the fifth patient was opened for fixing, the head of a Teutonic knight popped out in a spiked helmet, and shouted, 'Wiederausrustung!' (This, I am told, translates as 're-armament'.) That shows how Spike felt about his battles!

More recently, I heard a story about Spike awake. I hadn't heard this story before, but I have to believe it because it came from the mouth of an Old Bailey judge.

A number of years ago Spike had had his house robbed twice in a very short period of time. Not much was stolen, but he felt that he was a victim, and that the burglars were assaulting the very heart of his personal sanctuary. He walked back and forth in the radio studio almost frothing at the mouth, suggesting he was going to wait for the villains to come back and blow them into little pieces. And he was convinced that they would come back again, for it did seem that there was a pattern to their crimes. Each of the other break-ins had occurred on the last Monday of the month. So, on the next final Monday, Spike armed himself and hid in the shrubbery in front of his house.

Most surprisingly, his instincts proved to be right; there, in the drizzle of the evening air, were two men at the side of his front path.

They came out of the shadows and looked around full of suspicion and caution. And then moved toward a window in his dark house. As they got ready to climb up on to the outside window-sill, Spike jumped out of the shrubbery, fired his gun and shouted, 'Got you!'

The villains were so surprised that they almost fainted. So the first thing they did was beg to surrender.

When they were brought into court the unthinkable happened. They were let off! As the judge explained, 'Since the accused did not enter the Milligan property, and there is no evidence they intended to gain illegal access, the charge of breaking and entering is dismissed. Since it is not necessarily against the law to look in a window, and we have no witness to or evidence of trespass, all other charges are dismissed. However, while I know that you, Mr Milligan, were armed only with an air rifle — air rifle or no — I am forced to fine you a hundred pounds for the discharge of an offensive weapon.'

I could visualize all of this in a Goon script. Spike would turn to the burglars and shout, 'Let that be a lesson to you, varlets. Next time you come to my house you will hang!'

I don't think he should ever be described as a violent man — though for a period in his life he was a champion thrower when frustrated or angry. Even when he was in one of those occasional fits of temper, there was always the sense that there was a line he wouldn't cross — like some pub brawler, who would stop after the emotional release of the first easy punch. I am sure that much of Spike's reputation for temper comes from his face. Spike has always had a profound talent for looking demented.

I remember that once, in the 1950s, a young man at the BBC came rushing up to me, with his face ashen, and whispered that he had heard that Spike had gone over to Peter's apartment with a gun. I am not sure of any details beyond that, or even that this gun business ever really happened. I have no idea what the argument was supposed to be about, either. But I do remember my reaction. I extended my hands in front of me, palms up, rolled my eyes to the heavens and said, 'Oh yeah! So what else is new?'

Couldn't someone have been killed? Or hurt? At the very least, couldn't it have ended their relationship? Not a chance! Hurting each other wasn't part of the game. The next day the two of them were sitting at a table eating crisps and talking about shoes. It seemed that Spike's wife had thrown out all his scuffed-up, comfortable old footwear. He was now about to go on stage and do the show in slippers. Borrowed from Peter.

The most private times Spike and I spent together were in my car. We would be on our way to do a show in a theatre out of town somewhere, and since Spike had not then learned to drive he would hitch a ride with me. Often he would sit there and grumble the whole time. He would talk about the other two Goons as 'Secombe' and 'Sellers', although he always spoke to them direct as 'Harry' and 'Pete'. He would talk about them in a way that was so antagonostic that a stranger might feel that he could hardly wait to get back at the bastards. But that wasn't what it was about.

It was as though he was talking to a brother about another brother. God help someone else if they thought that gave them licence to start criticizing too! It was sometimes a strange loyalty he had to Peter and Harry. Or, maybe it was, indeed, a brotherly love.

I cannot recall even one occasion where there was a cruel bite or violence in the thought behind his comedy writing. Instead there was always whimsy, gentleness, innocence and — especially — the absurd. Here is an example from the BBC Anniversary Show in 1972:

PETER: 'Here we are starving to death and all you can think of is food!'

ANNOUNCER: 'Two people are dealing with a moot point.'

PETER: 'Don't you point that moot at me!'

HARRY: 'The uniform has to go back. There's a deposit on it.'

SPIKE: 'I'll brush it off.'

When I read those lines on paper I still find them amusing — maybe silly — but they don't seem brilliantly funny. But if you had been there in the audience in 1972, or heard the show on radio, you would have heard the reaction of people in Goon heaven.

It was Peter and Spike who developed the characters and fleshed them out on the Goon Show. And, especially, it was Peter. Peter was so versatile that if Spike happened to be absent, he could play his own and Spike's characters too. That meant nearly all the voices!

But if Spike wasn't versatile in that way, his gift was that he could always hear and see the characters in his mind. He seemed to know just how the lines would sound on the air. And because of this he always seemed to be able to adapt the lines — perfectly and appropriately — to the character who was saying them.

I remember that I once heard George Burns talking about Gracie Allen: 'Gracie never said funny things, she said things funny.' Spike knew his characters so well that he could make them do both. I think that is why so many of the recurrent expressions of Bluebottle and Min and Seagoon became such well-loved running jokes for the audience.

I would sit there at the edge of the stage and listen to these Goon characters who were like old friends. And then suddenly there it would be, an old familiar line and almost at the same instant the convulsive laughter would begin. I had heard those lines a hundred times, but I would find myself caught up in the infectiousness — and the laughter would go on and on and on.

When I saw Spike a couple of years ago in London, the

only complaint he had about life was to do with work, which he expressed as a complaint that 'those guys don't use me any more'. I'm not sure which guys he meant — he still appears a great deal and is, after all, a best-selling author. He has certainly not been forgotten — and I would measure his success another way. I would measure it by the way his work has endured. Forty years and still going strong.

There was always speculation about whether the Goons were extra-terrestrial, slightly demented, or whether they were continuously bombed on pills or booze. I have had people say to my face that they know 'for a fact' that everyone on the show was drunk. This comes from the school of thinking which believes that you can only find creative craziness in some kind of container. Well, the Goons did find it in a container. It was called a skull!

During the whole of the show's ten years I never saw any of them drunk on the show. They were too professional, and the show was too important to them, to try and perform half-cut. And if you listen to their incredible timing, their very precise articulated speech under those heavy comic voices, their control of themselves is self-evident. Besides, Spike Milligan would never have allowed anyone to muck up his brainchild. In fact, very often he would shout at Peter after the show, if Peter had had one of his fits of giggling and hadn't been able to control his performance.

That is not to say they did not drink at all! If you listen carefully to some of the programmes, when the musical interlude comes and I am introduced, you will hear a voice in the background saying something like, 'Around the back there for the old brandy!' It was a clarion call to imbibe a concoction of alcohol and milk — a combination which Harry Secombe introduced to the group. So, as far as the Goon Show is concerned, it can be claimed that I was a cue for the very first 'pause that refreshes' on radio.

I never indulged in the brandy and milk on the show, because it was my policy not to take even one drink on the day of a performance. This might lead you to the conclusion that I was Mr Squeaky-clean. Alas, it is not so.

I have never drunk excessively. I would have a little wine, a little whisky and, once in a great while, drink a little beer, but never very much. But there was a time when I did become excessive about something else.

Throughout the 1930s, 40s and 50s, marijuana seemed to be the drug of choice among many of the musicians I knew. I had started smoking it in the days before the war, when I was in Paris with Ray Ventura's band. We called it *mauvaise* — which was short for *mauvaise herbe*. That means 'weed' in French. It was illegal, but nobody paid much attention to what the crazy musicians were doing. And as long as we didn't get into heavy drugs like heroin, no one bothered us.

In the England of the 1950s, while they were far from being innocents, Peter, Spike and Harry would have been appalled at the prospect of using pot themselves. But I still did. As most self-justifiers are apt to say: 'Mind you, I didn't abuse it, or use it regularly! Just quite a bit, quite often.' (Since I now work at the Betty Ford Center, some people are going to interpret this as an evangelical message about the evils of alcohol and drugs! It may be that message to some, and I do not apologise for that. But the reason I want to tell you this story is because it was a moment in my life when I learned something about the way I behaved. And about my need to be in control.)

Ever since I first learned to play the harmonica, I have always been unsatisfied with the results: always critical that my playing wasn't the perfect performance that I wanted. At the same time, I take great pride in my talent, and standards are very precious to me. On one of the Goon Shows both my pot policy and my standards slipped.

One Sunday I did something I had never done before: I smoked pot on a show day. During the recording of the programme I was still stoned. After I had finished playing, my reaction was that I had finally done it — my best performance! Then, when I heard the recording of the show on the air, I couldn't believe it. It was rubbish. I never again tried to perform after smoking pot.

About eight months after that, I had my second lesson. Spike invited a gang of people, including Peter and me, to come over to his house to celebrate the third birthday of his daughter. That was a very natural thing for Spike to do, for Spike never thought of children as being something separate and apart from adults. I think that is why when he writes children's books they are such a great success.

During the course of the party I sneaked outside and smoked a joint, and found myself high and happy. Then it was time for fireworks, and so the entire party moved outdoors. Spike had bought a large box of splendid rockets that would climb high in the sky and burst into a shower of colour.

We all stood there, enjoying it. And then one of the rockets failed — it rose only a few feet and then dropped, spluttering, to the ground. Spike's three-year-old daughter wandered over for a closer look. The other adults were standing on the far side, so I was the closest person to her. But I didn't move in her direction — I just stood there, paralysed. Then I took a couple of steps backward, and put my hand over my eyes to protect myself.

Evidently someone else ran forward and scooped her up. The rocket never did go off, and little Miss Milligan wasn't hurt in the least. For which I thank God. But I was so ashamed, and so disappointed with myself, that I never touched that stuff again after that.

Over the years there have been many learned treatises written about the Goon Show. There are recurrent suggestions that the Goon comedy is rooted in Lewis Carroll, or the Marx Brothers, or the English music hall, or film cartoons like Loony Toons. But what I have seen — over the ten years I was with the show and in the almost forty years I have known those people — makes me think that the comedy was really rooted in the Goons themselves.

Away from the programme, Spike Milligan, Michael Bentine and Harry Secombe were all marvellous story tellers. But the nature of the stories each told — the subjects they talked about and the way they told them — was quite different.

Spike would tell stories that were full of quick wit, farce and satire. Michael Bentine, on the other hand, was the raconteur. He had the best formal education of anyone in the group, and perhaps was the most intellectual, so his language and imagery were splendid. But his humour was not always high flown, sometimes it bordered on the silly. Sometimes, as far as Michael was concerned, the sillier the better. And Michael seemed to find boundless boyish joy in just telling the story. But the stories were always full of people and insight and humanity too, because Michael is a gentle man.

Peter Sellers was generally the most serious of the group. I would describe Peter as someone who loved fun, but didn't especially enjoy jokes. However, he could be devastatingly funny when he burlesqued someone. He became a comic entertainer partly because he joined the Air Force, and ended up in an entertainment unit. Spike had the same experience, coming from the Army. And it turned out that Harry came from the Army this way too.

Harry left Swansea to join the Army some time in 1940, when he was barely eighteen. He ended up in North Africa. During this time, he met a young Irishman by the name of Milligan.

As a lance-bombadier, Harry's job was to fire artillery pieces. It is recorded that he was less than successful for, when he dug down into his vocal reservoir and gave an order to fire, he could be heard over the guns on both sides of the line. It was felt that this took all the surprise out of it for the Germans.

I don't have any idea whether or not the two events are related, but Harry was transferred to an entertainment unit in the Army.

His Army act was pure music hall. It included a singing duet, with Harry doing both parts of the song 'Sweethearts', made famous I think by film musical stars Jeannette MacDonald and Nelson Eddy. In Harry's version, the bitter-sweet, star-crossed romantic tragedy is augmented by a lover's quarrel. The song lyrics contain the line: 'When we were lovers in June'. The soprano voice seemed to think it might have been May! There was a confrontation between the duetting pair, and the act ended with a raspberry and someone getting a finger in the eye.

I remember him telling me about another act he did in those

Army days. It was a shaving routine which was mostly pantomime. In it Harry demonstrated all the aspects of the male shaving ritual, and ended up drinking the shaving water. Knowing that this was done before the days of aerosol cans of whipping cream, I asked him what he had used. He looked at me blankly and asked, 'What do you mean?' 'Well,' I said, 'you were trying to look as though you were shaving, did you use egg whites or something?' 'Shaving cream!' he replied. There was a very long pause. Then he added, 'I suppose it is an acquired taste!'

I don't know exactly when all the Goons met, but by the time 'Crazy People' came along they had known each other and had worked with each other on radio a number of times.

I cannot talk about Harry for very long without bringing up the subject of his family. If Harry was somewhat different from the other Goons in his approach to comedy, he was also different from them in his personal style of life. Harry was the first of all the Goons to be married. As you might expect he married a Welsh girl — a smiling, laughing, lovely lady who built a relationship with Harry that was always meant to last a lifetime. Myra and Harry were the first to buy a home, the first to have children (they have four), and the first to settle into something resembling a secure and structured life.

It sometimes seemed odd that this madcap man could be so peaceful and gentle in his home. But then, a large part of Harry always seemed to need the life of a home-body — a man whose home was his castle, and his family his universe. You can see where it comes from when you read his book *Goon Abroad*, for Harry speaks lovingly of his childhood experiences in Swansea, and describes them as among the most vivid in his life. 'I have never really left Swansea,' he says. 'I have taken it with me.'

Although Harry was always very giving and always a vital part of the Goons, he carefully preserved a large portion of his personal life and kept it separate.

If I try to sum up this dear friend, I would say that the overriding trait of all Harry's traits was always his great humility. I think the audience sensed both his shyness and humility from the very first — and it is one of the reasons that

Harry is perhaps the best loved of all the Goons. It is odd how these traits often combine into the making of the world's best clowns — for as a comedian that is exactly what Harry Secombe is. Of all the Goons, it was he who was by far and away the greatest lover of jokes, and he who was most likely to start clowning.

Perhaps he has always felt the need to perform: I can remember going out to dinner, and even as we entered the restaurant he would start. Harry might go round to all the patrons in the place and introduce himself as 'Secombe here!' Then he would come back to the table, attach a dinner plate to his forehead — where it would rest in place as though held on by superglue — and, as the whole room looked on, shout out, 'If this does a tumble we all die!' Then he would sit down quietly and we would have dinner together. And he would become quietly entertaining. And be an endearingly good listener.

We once talked about his curious use of glasses. Although he always had his glasses on when he did a radio broadcast and had to read a script, he would seldom wear them if he was singing, or doing a set skit on stage. When I first noticed it, I thought it might be vanity — but it wasn't!

Harry had measles as a child, and it left his eyesight permanently weakened, so that he has been short-sighted throughout his life. When he started his career on stage he left his glasses off and used this as his shield. As Harry said, 'I can't see them, you see! I can hear them, mind, and I can sometimes smell the garlic. But, as they say — they must all be drunk out there, because they sure look blurry to me! I just pretend all the blokes are smiling and all the women are topless. I have a wonderful time.'

Harry was always extremely sensitive about his singing, and often very insecure. I can remember him saying to me, many, many times over the years, 'How do you like my singing?'

The truth is that he had a powerful, rich voice but that there were times when he couldn't quite take it seriously. In fact it wasn't until 1950, and the show 'Welsh Rarebit', that he agreed to do his first serious solo on the radio. Up until then, when he sang he would clown.

I remember a charity benefit where he and I were asked to perform. Harry was asked to sing a song very straight. It was in a large, lush theatre, and the audience was a sedate group of money-bags, dressed up in evening gowns and dinner jackets. After a very formal introduction, Mr Secombe came out and sang 'Only Make Believe'. He did a lovely job all the way through the song, until the very end.

On the word 'do', in the final line 'But to tell the truth, I do', the singer has the option of going down the scale, or up the scale. However, there are rules to go with the up or the down! Harry couldn't seem to find the rules, or a pitch or a key he liked. He tried sliding through several. As about two thousand of us held our breath, Harry gave off a resounding 'do' and fell straight back — as flat and stiff as a board. The audience roared.

I have never understood how he could fall like that, and not split open his head. However, as he has grown older he has stopped doing that pratfall.

In 1987, I appeared as a guest on Harry's television programme *Highway*. It was delightful to appear with Harry once again, and to hear that his marvellous voice had only improved with the years.

I once did a count of how many Goon shows we had done and I seem to recall the total was around 207. That doesn't include the radio specials or the television shows. So you see, over the decade, there had been a large amount of Goon and Goon-like programming. But by the time the 1960s arrived I think we all felt that the Goons had run their course. At the same time, after the last show ('The Last Smoking Seagoons' on 28 January 1960) we also knew that we would be missing something from our lives. On the last show we were also missing Secombe. Harry was ill. Knowing Harry, it was probably an acute attack of emotion!

9

Peter Sellers

OF ALL THE things that made the Goon Show decade special, the friendship I formed with Peter Sellers is probably the most important.

Peter was the only one of the Goons who had a show-business family. On his mother's side of the family, the Rays had a history in English musical reviews which went back almost two hundred years. It wasn't that the Rays were stars or luminaries from the theatre: they were curtain pullers, jugglers, singers, piano players, and sometimes they were the managers of the place. The result was that Peter's family was always ready to encourage him, and when his mother, Peg Ray Sellers, recognized the slightest possibility that Peter might achieve success, she was there to push him toward it.

Peter's father was a small, quiet man from Yorkshire, who spent most of his family life in the background. But he too had worked for a while in the theatre — playing the piano and singing comic songs — and, evidently, he too shared the hope of having Peter in the business. But Peter didn't start off as the performer you might expect.

When he was about seven years old he was described by an aunt as 'the noisiest child in the district.' His mother preferred to describe him as 'a creative and sensitive child, who was exploring his talent'. The reason for this difference of outlook lay in the fact that Peter seemed obsessed with banging away at pots and pans. He would line them up, in the fashion of different-sized kettledrums, and bash away with a set of whittled-down legs from an old table. At his mother's insistence, and to get the pans back on the stove, his father bought him a beginner's set of drums.

There is a family story that if you had gone up to Peter and asked him almost any question: 'How is school?' — 'How do you feel?' — 'Where are you going?' — 'What would you like for supper?' — his answer would have been, 'I want to be a drummer.' The family may have thought it was just a stage he was going through, but it turned out that he took the whole business of drumming very, very seriously. It was a love which was to stay with him throughout his whole life. And it turned out that he did begin his show-business career drumming.

When he was barely a teenager, his uncle, Bert Ray, came along and offered him a job in a theatre he was managing. This variety house had an opening in the pit band, which played behind all the acts.

Now a drummer in a pit band of this type was required to play everything at more or less the same tempo, and his solo musical expression was pretty well reduced to those drum rolls and stings they play for acrobats, comedians and musicians. So, for young Peter, it was a creative musical experience equal to being back at the pots and pans. But he persisted, and had his first real taste of the stage, and sense of what seemed to entertain an audience. Soon he branched out and was playing drums with several small bands. He did all this long before he was eighteen.

Very close to his eighteenth birthday he joined the RAF, and it looked as though his musical career was about to be shelved for a few years. But he was only in the Air Force a very short time before he was reassigned from aircrew training to an entertainment unit in the RAF.

I have heard different stories about his reassignment in the RAF; that it had something to do with a slight heart murmur, or with his education, or that his feet were flat, or that he was afraid of heights, or that his arms were too long. I don't know which is true, but the one I prefer has to do with flying.

The story goes that one day, while Peter was in training, he went along on a flight as an observer. The crew was very relaxed, and they were making some rather rude comments

over the intercom about the sex life of one of the senior
officers and his ultra-fat wife. Peter came on the intercom
and, in a voice identical to that of the Squadron Leader,
suggested harsh punishments — which very nearly caused
the nervous crew to crash.

Whatever the real reason, he was seconded to a group
called 'Ralph Reader's RAF Gang Show'. And it was here
that he started to do more than play the drums. He did
impressions, and voices, and silly characters — which
weren't going to cause any crashes. He was a big success in
the Air Force!

But when he got out of the RAF, after the war, he had a
fairly rough time finding work. Wally Stott, who later
became the musical arranger for the entire series of Goon
Shows, and, after the second year, also conducted the
orchestra, told me how he once saw Peter standing in Archer
Street, the narrow street just behind the famous ('We never
close') Windmill theatre — where musicians used to hang
out and exchange news about jobs — dressed in his RAF
uniform, with his drums under his arms. Though Peter was
friendly enough, in a puppy-dog sort of way, he looked very
down to Wally, like someone who was about to throw in the
towel. But that was not Peter's way. He had other ideas, and
decided that if he didn't want to starve to death, he would
have to think of something better than being a drummer.

I mentioned that his mother's family, the Rays, were
connected with the theatre business. Well, for the second
time in his life, one of his uncles got him a job in a theatre
he was managing — this time in Peterborough. Peter was
very excited, because it was almost the first job he had had
in over six months. He was hired for a minor part in a
comedy/variety act. It turned into a disaster. Out of
nervousness and insecurity, Peter played his part very
straight and somewhat theatrically. He was booed off the
stage.

Peter was crushed by this reception, and was all ready to
go back to the drums, or even to give up the entire thought
of show business. But out of nowhere his good luck came
back. Somehow he was called about another job, and

although it was only a short-term booking, amazingly it was in London at the Windmill. As the saying goes, he was able to get right back up on the horse that bit him. This time there were no boos.

I think it was around the period of the Windmill booking that Peter met Spike and Harry and Michael. I once asked Michael and Spike what drew them to Peter and, without a pause, one of them said, 'Because he had talent!' The other said, 'His haircut.'

I am going to digress for a moment and talk about hair — because hair had much to do with the Goons in the early days. Among the photographs in this book you will see a picture of Harry, Spike, Michael and Peter. In it you will see hair on an epic scale. Perhaps you might believe that they are wearing wigs, or have teased and back-combed their hair to make it look like a ZsaZsa Gabor festival. In fact, this is not the case. The hair you see is entirely their own.

Harry Secombe always looked as though someone was holding the business end of a mop upright, with long strands of thick brownish stuff hanging down over the handle.

Michael Bentine looked as though his parents had invented hair. And since, even at the most illogical opportunity, he would tell you that he was half Peruvian, I am certain that he was cross-bred with one of those alpacas or vicuñas, or whatever it is they call those woolly things in the Peruvian mountains.

Spike seemed to have hair everywhere; except for a tiny patch on the tip of his nose and two small, round bare patches where his cheeks were. He once assured me that he was so hirsuit that hair grew directly out of his ears. This may account for his constantly saying 'Eh?'

The hair on his scalp resembled an ill-fitting Woolworth wig, made for a triple-X head size. The wig also appeared to have been left unattended in the bottom of a cage.

Peter's hair was much the most conservative of the group. It was cut short at the back and over his ears, and left ultra-thick at the sides. It looked home cut — by a designer who was trying to create hair-wings.

As for myself, I too had thick luxuriant hair. As an example to the others, I went out of my way to pay a Mayfair barber exorbitant amounts to cut my locks. As well as cutting them to be neat, my hairdresser also styled my hair by plastering it down with pounds of brilliantine. I ended up looking like a Dutch version of Rudolph Valentino. Unfortunately, while I had the Valentino hair, I still had the Barry Manilow nose.

I suppose, while I am talking about hair I must also make mention of noses. Goonophiles will recall that many, many programmes contained a reference to conks. Guess whose? I paid no attention to these references, because I always though of it as a patrician nose. But I can remember one of them saying to me, 'Just think, if you had your mother's features, everyone could say that you have a Maxie-mum nose!'

Terrible joke — nice nose.

In the late 1940s and early 1950s you had to appear on the radio if you were going to build a new career. And that meant the BBC. The music halls were losing most of their influence, and radio was the place that was creating the new stars. By the time I met him for the first time at the trial recording of Pat Dixon's 'Crazy People', Peter had done dozens of shows on radio, and made a name for himself.

We hardly said a word to each other that time; in fact we hardly spoke during the first three shows. It wasn't until the cast began going out for dinner, after the Sunday recording, that we started to have any kind of conversation. Then, suddenly, Peter and I began to feel very comfortable in each other's company. And gradually we grew closer and closer, until we became each other's best friend.

I didn't have to know Peter very long to realize that there were two things in life which were most important: performing and his mother. You can't really talk about Peter Sellers and not talk about Elizabeth Ray Sellers, his mother. She was a little woman, whom everyone, including Peter, called Peg. Somehow that kind of informality suggests she was a quiet, friendly person — in fact, she was rather feisty and scrappy. Above all, she doted on Peter. And when you were with them, her influence on him was very hard to miss.

There is a story about Peg and Peter while he was in the Air Force. Being with an entertainment unit meant that Peter was based in one place, so his mother decided that she and the family were going to move to a flat nearby. Almost every day after that, Peter would sneak home for lunch.

People have laughed about that, perhaps believing that he was just another hen-pecked mother's boy, but I don't think that is entirely true. I didn't know the Sellers family during the war, but later on I often saw them together at Peter's house or at his mother's flat. I sat there and heard Peg and Peter together — laughing, having some tea and a chat, or having a serious discussion about something important to them. I was never aware of the kind of domination you might see in an over-doting and over-protective mother, although I have to believe that, in his younger years, that might have been the case. During our times together I often heard them argue. The way he sometimes ignored her advice wasn't the behaviour of a milksop son. And, in fairness to Peg, Peter was her whole world. If she tried to nurture his talent, she also understood his weaknesses.

Michael Bentine was with us on the Goon show for the first two years, but he had been a good friend of Peter's for some time before that. I once asked Michael about Peg and Peter, and he suggested that it was Peg who was the 'special someone' Peter needed when he was beginning his life. Someone who gave him the faith and the confidence to believe in his talent; so that he could, in Peg's words, 'Make something of his gift.'

'Without Peg,' said Michael, 'I don't know that he would ever have got started. She didn't just praise him, she gave him a sense of what to do with his talent. You see, Peter certainly wasn't much to look at when I met him. And although you could tell he was talented, you couldn't tell whether he had anything to go with it. His mother was a very clever and intuitive lady.'

But there was one aspect of Peter's life where Peg wasn't always fair, and wasn't always right. It is a weakness of the

doting mother that no girl is good enough for her son. But
Peter always seemed to have a blind eye when it came to
noticing how Peg treated other women. And when he did
notice, the fact always seemed to surprise him.

I remember Peter telling me about being seventeen and
bringing home a well-built and smashing-looking redhead.
After all this time I can't remember her name, but I do recall
that it was one of those cutesy nicknames that some girls
give themselves. For the sake of identification we'll call her
Joan.

When Peter took Joan home there was cake and tea,
pleasant conversation and constant smiles. The meeting, he
thought, went extremely well. When Peter and Joan were
out of the door, however, Joan suddenly said, quite out of
the blue, 'Your Ma doesn't like me.' Peter was amazed.

When he was telling me this story he said, 'You know,
Max, it taught me that women have some sensory thing, like
ESP, between them.' It was something he would come to
believe in strongly, later in his life. And it was something
which affected, very directly, one of his later marriages.

I knew a man who used to tell this joke on himself:
marriage, he would say, was very important to him — it
must have been, because he did it so often. And then he
would laugh loudly, as though this was truly funny. I don't
know why he told that joke so often, and I don't know why
he seemed so tickled by the humour. Perhaps he really didn't
give a damn. At the same time I do know that a great many
of us try to laugh at, and dismiss, things which hurt us.

Peter was married a number of times, and he used to say,
in a very self-deprecating way, 'I've met another one who's
too good for me!' I don't think he liked his marital record,
but it was his first marriage which caused him most regrets.

I met all Peter's wives, but I knew him best at the time of
his first marriage, and that is the one I want to talk about. It
was in the late 1940s that the fates brought Ann into his life.
Of all the women in Peter's life, before and after Ann, I think
Peg, perhaps grudgingly, liked her best. But, more
importantly, I think Peter did too.

Peg was true to form with Ann: she wasn't good enough

for Peter! At this point Ann was an absolutely stunning young actress, who had the look of what we have come to call 'an English rose'. (A phrase, incidentally, which she detests.) She also had surprising style and poise for someone so young. Meanwhile, Peter Sellers was a man beginning to establish a reputation, but he wasn't much to look at! So, while Ann liked him, she wasn't exactly overwhelmed.

But Peter had become very smitten with her, and decided the way to capture her heart was to give her his undivided attention. In fact, he seemed to have nothing else on his mind.

He would telephone her, call for her, wait for her, and at parties never let her out of his sight. He would invite her to his performances, and ensure that she saw the way the audiences loved him. He wrote her notes, and sent her posies, and tried his best to cut a romantic figure. He even went to the length of locking her in a cupboard, and telling her he would never let her out unless she married him, and promised never to speak to another man in her entire life. She went along with the first half of that proposition.

But after they were married his behaviour was the opposite of all that. He was inattentive, preoccupied and often thoughtless. He would go away and forget she existed. Then he would be remorseful — but only for a day. When the children came along, he gave them a lovely home and luxuries, but not much of himself. And the part he gave to Ann became less and less, too, until there was nothing left between them. At this point in his life someone said of him, 'Peter Sellers will give you anything, except five minutes of himself.' That comment amazed me, because it was never true in our friendship. And yet, with some people in his life, I can see that it was true.

The irony is that after Ann and Peter were divorced he wanted her close to him. He sought her advice; he phoned often to assure himself that she was well; he bought her expensive presents which really showed affection; and he would often talk about her to other people. Ann told me that the presents and the attention continued long after she was remarried, and that it was often embarrassing to her and her new husband. But only once did Peter tell her, as he was walking out of the door, 'I made a mistake with you!'

Peter married three times after his marriage to Ann. And there were other women — including Sophia Loren and Liza Minelli — that, at one time or another, he would have liked to marry. They were all talented, exciting and generally startlingly attractive women. But, somehow, if you wanted all of him, Peter gave you nothing.

There was a great similarity in Peter's behaviour and the way his mother behaved towards people. Ann once described Peg as an absolute bloody terror as a mother-in-law. 'And yet,' she said, 'after Peter and I were divorced, and I was out of his life, she was almost a friend.'

Peg lived well into the years of Peter's movie stardom. After she died I once spoke to him about her; that was in California in the early 1970s. I said that I was sorry I hadn't heard about her illness until she was gone. He simply said, 'Yeah,' and looked down; he didn't raise his head for a very long time. Then he said, 'I don't know what I'll do without her. She always helped me do the right thing!' There was another pause and then, 'But I still talk to her!'

I think his mother's death was the start of Peter's need to believe in the spiritualist's world of palmists, fortune-tellers, seers and prophets, a world he seemed wholly to embrace when a mystic told him he was going to meet a wonderful woman with the initials B.E. A few months later he met, and married, Britt Ekland. In many respects Peter and I were an unlikely combination. I was ten years older, at a time in our lives when that many years could be a major gulf between people. I was a Dutch harmonica player and I had lived most of my life far from my family. I wasn't sophisticated or well educated, but I'd been on my own from the age of seventeen, in Brussels and Paris and London. I had been in a war. I had seen and lost a lot of things.

Peter had spent most of his life in London, and had very close family ties. He had never really been outside England. He was a very simply educated man, someone without a worldly bone in his body. And he was a comedian and an impressionist. How did we become friends?

You don't have to be very wise to know that friendship is always something complex, but if I was to describe, in a single word, why Peter and I became very close, that word would be 'trust'. Both Peter and I were very shy inside, very insecure about our talents, and achingly aware of our limitations in reaching out to other people. We both trusted each other with that secret.

I mentioned that Peter wasn't very much to look at when I first met him in 1950. If you have any memories of him in the film *The Lady Killers* then you have a very accurate picture of the way Peter was in life at that time. I remember that he once told me about an ancestor of his, the boxer Daniel Mendoza, who was a great bare-knuckle champion in the eighteenth century. The family story was that Peter looked very much like the famous pugilist. Certainly, in the 1950s, Peter might have been mistaken for a fighter. He was very swarthy and carried a lot of weight. And, although he didn't give the impression of being especially aggressive, he did look like someone who was just about ready to leap, full-force, into petty crime. Or, as the English expression goes, he looked something of 'a wide boy'.

He didn't have much social or physical grace either. He looked and acted more the rough and common bloke. Many people don't realize it but, while Peter wasn't particularly tall, he had a very big frame. Since he was very heavy at that time, his neck looked short and thick. Combined with that extra thick hair, this made him appear to have an immense head.

It was obvious he wasn't dim, but sometimes his shyness made it seem as though he was socially hesitant. And many people who met him in those days interpreted that as a sign that he didn't have enough social grace to know how to behave, when in fact he was such a marvellous social observer that, if he hadn't been so shy, even in those days he could have faked the behaviour of a duke.

But when one got to know him a little better, one didn't have to look very deep beneath the exterior to see other aspects of Peter. As well as his talent, there was something terribly likeable about him — that wide, boyish smile, together with a boyish sense of innocence. It is amazing that, as time passed, Peter grew more and more good-looking until, at one point in his life, he was leading-man handsome. And, while it was less, there still remained some of that innocence just below the surface.

Mind you, while he may have grown more handsome and polished and more successful, there was one aspect of his personality which never changed. Peter was a boy his entire life.

I realize I have to be careful when I say someone 'remained a boy', because people interpret it so differently. I am not talking about someone who is childish and immature — probably irresponsible and selfish. Peter Sellers was child-like: a very simple person in terms of some rather simple interests, and simple ways of thinking and feeling about things.

To begin with, Peter was never very complex intellectually. He didn't read very widely, and subjects such as politics, physics, mathematics and most of the social sciences were quite beyond his interest. But he did study people, and his observations and conclusions were very often shrewd and accurate.

Emotionally, he could be up or down, loud or quiet: most often that depended on who he was with. He could be very gregarious, or quite the opposite. In fact there were times when he was almost reclusive, and he would try to keep everyone away, irrespective of their relationship. At those times when people telephoned, he would always have someone else answer to tell the caller that he was in the shower. And sometimes he would not call back. I have been at his house and given such a message for him, and I've got it back over the telephone, too. Sometimes I would phone his house and when his wife, Ann, answered, I would ask, 'Is he in the shower?'

It wasn't that he hated the telephone, or was out of sorts, it was as though, at that moment, he couldn't communicate with people he couldn't see. Sometimes he wouldn't phone me back until the next day, or a few days later. He wouldn't actually apologize, but there was a sort of code between us. He would phone me and use my voice on the telephone. It was an unnerving experience to find myself talking to myself. Neither of us would comment on it, but we knew what it meant. He would keep it up for a while, and then Max/Peter would just fade away during the conversation. It was a very obscure apology.

There was one interest in Peter's life which I suppose you can describe as completely boyish. And it is one of the things that Peter and I shared closely. Some men play games, like golf or tennis or softball. Some join an athletic club, so they can lift and stretch and swim their hearts out. Some play poker or bingo, or go for the more intellectual pursuits of bridge or chess. Still others stick things in books or in glass cases. Half of the male population in England seems compelled to play in the garden, digging, pulling, planting and pruning, in plots the size of a postage stamp.

What Peter and I shared was a love of toys: children's toys and adult toys. We played with the intricate mechanical kind, and model trains, and other things that moved and crawled and flew and sparked and fired and banged. We even built things. Throughout our friendship we would go into toy shops and buy things for each other.

I can remember that one Christmas, when I was living in Los Angeles, I bought a mechanical toy helicopter for my very young son, Philip. When Peter came to the house I showed it to him and he said, 'I have got to have one of those.' And I reached behind and handed him a box. A nutty gift to give a movie star!

The novelty of the toys didn't last long, but while it did last the playtime was good time. I don't believe that something like this is silly, if it provides you with great joy. And I do know that we never seemed to play games where there had to be a winner. Quite often, like adults, we played at playing with the toys.

As Peter became more successful during the Goon years, and had the money, I shared the pleasure of his adult toys — his cameras, his sound systems and recorders, and, most of all, his many cars. He spent a fortune, or maybe two, on them.

He would phone me up and say, 'Ploog. I have seen a car.' And I would answer, in our ritual way, 'It's pretty good, is it? Then we'll have to go and see it.'

And when we saw it I would almost always say, 'Peter, you have to have that!'

After a while I became much more cautious with that stock saying, because in one of those years Peter ended up buying something in the region of sixteen cars. It's an astonishing number, especially when you consider that he never owned more than two at any one time. And this was long before he was a millionaire movie star.

His cars weren't to show off 'the latest and the best'. Peter was never like that. And it wasn't a need for an endless source of the exotic either, because I don't recall that any of them were in the Lamborghini Countach category. The buying was simply an impulse. I think it had a great deal to do with the fact that Peter loved to give and to receive gifts, too.

But the car business, like a great many other things in his life, was also based on the fact that Peter needed a world which was simple and uncomplicated. If his car had a dent or a scrape or a rattle, or something mechanically wrong, it was gone. And to Peter the business of waiting for things, and getting things fixed, was a complication. Things had to be perfect and dependable, and easy to cope with. But there was something of the 'new toy' syndrome too.

I remember a time when he took Ann and me to a car show. It seems to me that Peter had his eye on a Bentley. A gentleman dressed in a morning coat approached us. I cannot bring myself to refer to him by the lowly term 'salesman', so I shall refer to him as a Motor Vehicle Consultant. This MVC examined us to ensure we were worthwhile, and then suggested we were free to look at the automobile.

We examined it closely, inside and underneath. Then I stepped back to a rear wall, to take a full look at the Bentley in its environment. Meanwhile, Peter was being spoken to

by the consultant. When he approached me Peter said, with
enthusiasm, 'Don't you like it, Ploog?'

I was tempted to follow the usual pattern and say, 'You
have to have that!', but because of the Motor Vehicle
Consultant's treatment of us I said, 'I don't know, Peter. The
way it's designed I get the impression that it sags in the
middle.'

I didn't know that Peter had already arranged to buy the
car. But then he rushed up to the man in the morning coat,
took a paper from his hand, tore it up, and said, 'I can't have
that. I cannot have that.'

I am pleased to report that the man was non-plussed. For
a moment I regretted telling him about the sag, because I
thought he would be really disappointed. But, of course, it
didn't last. And the next week he had bought another car.

Michael Bentine and I used to chuckle about Peter and his
cameras and cars and gadgets. Michael once said that he had
thought of the perfect Christmas gift for someone with
Peter's attention span. 'A set of two thousand lead soldiers
depicting the Battle of Waterloo, which Peter could play
with for ten minutes, and then melt.'

No doubt his attention span made life much harder for
Peter later on, when he found himself living in the world of
a superstar. A world of too many choices, and so many
opportunities.

It has always seemed to me that some actors have the ability
to go beyond *playing* a part, to the point where they almost
become it. I have heard that as a description of the early work
of Orson Welles and Marlon Brando, and of actors like Meryl
Streep and Laurence Olivier. While Peter was not thought of
as a great dramatic actor, in many respects he shared that
ability to become another person. And sometimes, for the
people around him, it was a mixed blessing.

I remember once, early in his career, he had the lead in a
serious film where he played a small-time crook. When I
talked to his wife, Ann, she told me that he was being
absolutely impossible — that he was acting at home just the
way the script described him on the screen.

The picture, incidentally, was a flop. We went to see it together and he laughed and told me, 'I can't do those things! I'm faking! But I keep wanting to mug somebody.'

And I can remember another time, at the start of the 1960s, when Peter and Ann came to the 'Max is going away to America farewell party' at the home of my good friends Joe and Charlotte Robson. Peter was making a movie called *The Millionairess*, playing the part of a very Indian gentleman. That night he came straight from the set at the studio, and he arrived complete with make-up and costume. Ann was with him. As I was coming down the stairs he was going up, and he looked at me as though we were passing strangers. The only thing he did was to give me a slight wave of acknowledgement and bow of the head — the type an Indian might give to acknowledge a stranger.

Ann said, 'Well, you know what that is all about, Max. Pay no attention. Mahatma is making a picture.'

One might have thought that Peter had simply been having a little fun before he took off his costume and make-up, but the fact is that when Peter stepped into character he seemed to step out of Peter. As Ann said to me later, 'It's like being married to the United Nations.'

There is, however, one film where I don't feel he changed much of his own character to be the character. That was the film *Being There*. I can recall when I saw it, I said to my wife, Susan, 'There is a great deal of Peter in Chauncey Gardiner.'

Chauncey Gardiner is a wonderfully whimsical creation. In the film some characters see him as simple-minded, with nothing between the ears. By others he is thought to be simple to the point of genius.

While no one ever thought of Peter as simple-minded, there *were* particular qualities of simplicity about him. These included some peculiar fears and insecurities. There were things he sheltered himself from, or turned off in his mind.

I remember some time in the late 1950s, we were somewhere in the North of England making a stage appearance together, and it was very, very cold. As we often did, we arranged to stay in a hotel — not a very lavish hotel, in fact it fell into the category of lean-to when we had to endure its version of central heating. We liked to share a large room with two big beds, but this room was just about as freezing as the weather outside, because there was so much draught by the window-frame that a flag would have flown straight out.

That night Peter complained, 'Max, it's so cold in here, I'll never get warm! How can I do any work, when I'm so cold I can't sleep and I can't think?'

I said to him, 'Look, Pete, we can do something about this tomorrow. I've just bought myself an electric underblanket and I have it on my bed at home. They're new, and they're great. We'll get you one tomorrow!'

'I don't know, Max,' he said over and over. 'I don't know!'

The next morning I found a shop and bought an electric blanket for him. That night I presented it to him, and you could almost see him perspiring nervously. He kept walking back and forth across the room, wiping his glasses and putting them on again. 'Do you think it is safe, Ploog? Maybe I'll try it later! I don't want to fool with something electric!'

There was real apprehension in his voice.

Finally, I took the blanket and put it over the mattress and made the bed, but it still took me forty minutes before he was even close to lying down and trying it. Finally, he casually walked across the room and sat in a chair, as though he had made up his mind about something. He took a newspaper in his hand, and in a tone that was completely off-hand — as though it hadn't mattered even in the beginning — he said to me, 'OK, Ploog. If you think so.'

About two minutes later he lay on the bed and it was a joy to be there. Peter kept on saying, 'This is wonderful. Wonderful.' And he closed off the night by saying, 'I have to get one for Ann in the morning.'

He didn't forget. The next morning he bought two more. His and an extra were put in the boot of his car. Just in case I forgot mine.

Because we were on the radio regularly and were widely known, people tended to think that we were growing rich. The truth is that, while those first two years on the Goon Show were marvellous in terms of having regular work and exposure, the fee that the BBC paid amounted to about half a week's pay for the average clerk. It meant that we had to take advantage of our popularity, and do other work. And we all did.

One of the things I did was make records. I wish I could report that they were smashing sales successes, but they did other things for me instead. While I made little money, I had the chance to work with some tremendous people

In the mid-1950s, I made a record called 'Goon With the Wind', with tunes like 'Crazy Rhythm', 'It's Only a Paper Moon', 'Our Love is Here to Stay', 'Duke's Joke', written by Alan Clare, a wonderful pianist and a friend of long standing. I also recorded a tune I'd composed myself, called 'Chérie, Chérie'.

George Martin, who later worked with the Beatles, produced the record; the title of 'Goon With the Wind' was his idea, and I hope he won't mind my using it again for this book.

At the same time as I was recording, I was also doing tours with visiting stars from America. People like Bob Hope, Dinah Shore, Frank Sinatra, Johnny Rae with the Hi-Lo's, and a very young Sarah Vaughan. I made quite a bit of money this way, and it was pretty heady stuff. But the very best times were, no doubt, making appearances with the Goons.

We couldn't bill ourselves as 'The Goons', partly because that was a title preserved for the radio programme, and partly because we were almost never all together on the same bill. But it did seem that almost every Monday morning some combination of the Goons was going off somewhere to do a stage show, in some corner of England, Scotland or Wales. Mostly it would be Peter and I, Spike and I, Harry and Peter and I, or whatever other combinations you can make out of the names.

The constant 'and I' part of it was because it was much

better to balance a comedian or comedians, with a musical act, rather than bill the comedy alone. Besides, they could use me as a straight man, whom no one expected to be funny.

You wouldn't work with people like Peter, Spike, Michael and Harry without learning a great deal about audiences and working an audience. All four of them seemed to have an uncanny sense. They could look out from behind the curtain, or take the few seconds while they were walking to the centre of the stage, and instinctively know how the audience was going to react to them.

Michael Bentine would get that audience sense and then alter his timing — making the tempo of his act faster or slower. Of course words like 'faster' and 'slower' are relative when you speak of Michael. The amount of energy he put into everything was always equivalent to a beehive full of ten-foot bees. Perhaps I would be more accurate if I said that Michael would decide to be more manic or less manic.

Michael was always the most cerebral of the Goons. One moment he would be terribly articulate, urbane and cultured. The next he would do falling-down burlesque. He was someone who could have gone on to be one of the thinking-man's Three Stooges. Mind you, that person would have had to be a very mad thinking-man.

On the other hand, Peter's approach to his audience was quite different. Peter never wanted to go on stage as Peter Sellers. And so a little while before he was due to go on stage (and often during the time I was on with my act) he would stand in the wings and stare at the audience. He would stand there and decide who he should be!

Then he would go somewhere and get some props, and dream up something to go with them. The props might be old bits of clothing, bits of make-up, an old shawl, a carpet, a picture frame. They were sometimes unusual props, and sometimes they were a bit outlandish.

Quite often, near the end of my act, he would simply walk, shuffle, or enter on his knees, unannounced. Frequently the audience wouldn't twig that it was him. There he was on the bill, and people knew about him and his characters, but he was just so good that they were never sure.

There is one time in particular I remember, because the story has such an extraordinary ending. It was at the Hippodrome Theatre in Wolverhampton. At one time the Hippodrome had been a very elegant theatre, but by the 1950s it was beginning to look a little dilapidated. Still, they paid fairly decent money and had pretty large crowds, so it was a good place to work. On this occasion I was on the stage, in the process of introducing my final number, when Peter made one of those anonymous entrances.

He was dressed up in work-boots, a little cap, a cardigan and great baggy canvas trousers. He shuffled along, stooped over as though he were a man in his late seventies. He walked past the edge of the curtain to the apron of the stage, and stood there. I ignored him at first, but I could tell the audience was no longer concentrating on me. They were wondering who the old bird was at the side of the stage.

Finally I said, 'Excuse me, we're doing a show here, could you go somewhere else!'

He shuffled and looked embarrassed. 'Sorry, sir, but I have to tell you something important. There's no danger mind you, but there is a fire drill next door.'

'Oh, my God,' I thought, 'he's going to clear the theatre with a fire drill!' But he didn't.

Peter seemed to hesitate, then he turned slightly, as though he was going to walk off the stage. But he turned back again and said, 'The Chief of the Fire Brigade wants to come in and talk for a moment. I thought you was finished, sir. I'm sorry.'

With that he proceeded to come towards me, and now we could see that he was trailing a fire-hose. He handed me the nozzle (pointed in the direction of the audience) and said 'I'll get 'im.' Half the audience knew. The other half wasn't sure.

A man in the front row shouted, 'Would you point that thing somewhere else?' And I said to my offstage friend, 'You aren't going to turn that thing on now, are you?'

I stood there on stage, not knowing what to do, but reacting with the audience by throwing up my hands at this interruption. Finally Peter reappeared in the black suit, belt, boots and silver helmet of the Fire Brigade. He skipped across the stage and proceeded to deliver a completely hysterical lecture. It was full of sexual innuendo on fire-hoses and fire prevention. It brought the house down.

His closing words were, 'I would like to thank you all for your attention. It is such a pleasure to deliver the message of fire prevention in such a luxurious temple to the Arts.' Then, he looked around and said, 'Come to think of it, this place could do with a good old burn-down!'

There is a tag to this story. I know it is going to sound like something a storyteller might add on when he is trying to give the story a better ending, but I swear to you it is true. Two days after we had finished our engagement, Peter phoned me and said, 'Ploog! I can't believe it. The bloody theatre in Wolverhampton burned down!'

Peter Sellers was always a true artist in the field of developing comic characters — or tragic ones for that matter! Several times I have heard him described as having a tape machine in his head, which he used to recall and imitate people at will. I think it was more than that. He didn't imitate them, he mirrored them. I have met many impressionists, and most of them are voice imitators who affect the broad gestures of a star — a John Wayne or a Katharine Hepburn, a current politician or a television host. Peter's characters were much more complex, as though he was able to distil all the facets of an archetype, and make it breathe as a human being. He could imitate people, but he could also create them.

You might ask, where did he get his inspiration? Well, I don't think any of his talent derived from anyone else. I do know that there were people he greatly admired and, in some respects, would have liked to model himself on.

One performer he admired was Sir Alec Guinness, whom he thought of as beyond superb. When he heard the news that they were going to be working together in *The Lady Killers*, he was about as excited and awe-struck as I have ever seen him.

They had never met, so when Guinness heard the news he called Peter and invited him over to his house for lunch. They got along very well. After they had finished the picture Peter told me that Guinness had been very helpful to him, and that he had learned a great deal. And he said, 'Max, you cannot believe how quiet this man is. He's shy!' Then he laughed and said, 'He's got a switch inside. He turns it on, and another person pops up!'

It is astonishing that this soft-spoken elegant man could be such a powerful focus for those around him. Peter and he were men of different temperaments, but I suppose there might have been a similarity between Guinness's internal fire — his turn-on switch — and Peter's. Later on Peter would sometimes do the Sellers version of Sir Alec, though I doubt it was ever in the presence of Guinness. They never really had much more than a casually-good friendship, but I think that Alec Guinness did have a lasting effect on Peter Sellers the actor.

Not all comedians love other comedians, but Peter, Spike and Harry did. At the head of the list of their idols and influences were the great stars of the silent pictures: Charlie Chaplin, Harold Lloyd, Harry Langdon, Charlie Chase and, most especially, Buster Keaton. And there was another performer whose only channel was sound — Mel Blanc, the voice of Bugs Bunny, Elmer Fudd and a thousand other Warner cartoon voices. Peter spent time with Harold Lloyd and Buster Keaton, but I remember an occasion when a very contemporary comedian was added to that list.

Peter and I went to see a French comedy called *Monsieur Hulot's Holiday*, which starred Jacques Tati. Having lived in Paris, I was pretty familiar with French cinema, but this was the first time I'd come across Tati's work. Almost immediately after its London showing everyone was saying he was a genius, and that the film was a comic masterpiece. The British are not much given to this form of description for a Frenchman!

There is a strange dead-pan vulnerability among some of the great silent comics — Buster Keaton being the prime example — and Tati had some of that same quality.

Monsieur Hulot's Holiday has sound, but in many ways it is like a silent film full of long periods without dialogue, full of pratfalls and mix-up scenes and visual humour which has intricate props and split-second timing. Peter talked about the film for a week, and then did something I had never known him to do before: he wrote to Tati and told him how much he thought of his work. The second surprise was that Tati replied almost straight away. It was one of those informal invitations that say '. . . if you are ever in the neighbourhood, drop in'. Although I wouldn't have expected it of him, Peter decided to visit France and meet the master.

When he came back after a few days he seemed very, very disappointed. He wouldn't say much about it at first, but then, over several weeks, the story came out.

They had met at someone's house, and sat around a table in the garden, drinking coffee. Then Tati had proceeded to lecture Peter about comedy, as though comedy was some theory based on an engineering study. And he did this in a tone which suggested to Peter that he was granting a papal audience.

Peter said, 'All he did was talk to me about how great he is. And about his comic theories. Ploog, the man has no sense of humour!'

Generally when Peter and I went on the road to do variety shows (vauderville in America), we would be booked from Monday to Saturday. Often on a Sunday, if we weren't recording a Goon Show, we would book a Sunday concert: the same act, but very often in a concert hall.

About three weeks after Peter's brush with Tati Peter and I were travelling on a Saturday evening. We were on our way to make one of those Sunday stage appearances. When we had booked into the hotel we decided to go and see a film, and there was Tati on the bill. Peter couldn't help himself: before the film was half over, Tati was back up on that pedestal reserved for Buster Keaton and the other great comedians he loved.

Some time after that Tati wrote to Peter to say that he had seen one of his pictures, but I don't believe that Peter ever replied. Sometimes it is better to keep the artist and the man separate.

Popular wisdom says that when radio is at its best, it is a visual medium. I take this to mean that the difference between television and radio is that radio allows you to create your own images in your mind. Radio is a matter of imagination. If you accept that, then it tells us a great deal about the performers on the Goon Show, and their talent for making characters 'visualizable'.

I read a newspaper column once which said that the characters that Peter and Spike played on the show were actually exaggerations of people the Goons had met. Since truth is mostly stranger than fiction, I suppose that could be true. But I tend to think the characters had parts from many people in them.

I have seen doodles and drawings of the characters, scribbled on the top of script pages. Spike seemed to do this more than anyone else.

But there was a form of silent consensus among the Goons that no pictures, or renderings of the characters, should be published. Spike felt very strongly that the characters should be left to the imaginations of the listeners. And so, when the *Radio Times* asked if they could publish some of the doodles, they were refused. Then someone at *Radio Times* came up with another strategy.

Some time toward the middle of the 1950s the BBC decided to ask the listeners to send along drawings of what *they* thought the Goon characters looked like. Not surprisingly, there were thousands of cartoon submissions. But what was surprising was the fact that, among all those thousands of Goon Show listeners, there was an astonishing similarity in the way they saw the characters. I cannot remember a single occasion where the script had any real description of what a character looked like — so the similarity in the way listeners saw the characters had to come from somewhere else.

I remember the first time we all sat down to look at piles of the drawings. Spike and Peter shouted out with great glee,

'They've got it!'

Secombe responded, 'I'll take them over to Nursey for shots!'

Returning to the question of how characters were created, I can tell you about one very famous film character that Peter developed. And it was indeed based on a real person.

Just before Peter was starting the first of the *Pink Panther* films, he and Michael Bentine had a talk about the role of Inspector Clouseau. The movie script was a very funny one, but it was not specific as to what this character was like and how it should be played. The producers had left it to Peter to invent Clouseau.

Michael reminded Peter about a man we had all met who was one of Princess Margaret's hairdressers. The gentleman in question had a very high-pitched and throaty voice. He also possessed a very distinctive French accent, with which he strangled, mauled and swallowed certain English vowel sounds. This is reflected in the way that Clouseau rendered the word 'moth' — which came out 'muhth'. Peter experimented for an hour or so, and then said he had found it. I am sure that Princess Margaret, who was a friend to both Peter and Michael, never guessed. But now you know. Clouseau is a former royal hairdresser.

I have often been asked 'Were the Goons close?' I think that if you purposely move closer to someone, it is a strong indication of emotional closeness. And for a couple of years several of us were not only personally close, but physically close as well.

Around the time of the second anniversary of The Goon Show I was still living in a bed-sitter. It was large enough, but it wasn't exactly 'homey'.

I started to save my money so that I could afford the luxury of a nice flat. I thought that even if I couldn't afford something with 'star status', at least I could find a place with a little twinkle. Anyway, I was fed up with the thirteen cats next door.

My problem was that, in the early 1950s, getting a place

in London that could reasonably be described as 'nice' was
the equivalent of being in the sciences and finding a cure
for death!

Mind you, there were ways. You could murder a maiden
aunt, and take over her lease. You could put yourself on a
waiting list, which might benefit your descendants. You
could bribe a slum landlord, with ninety per cent of your
worldly wealth. Or, you could be 'connected'. I ended up
being connected.

Peter's cousin was an estate agent and one day Peter came
to me and said, 'Ploog, we've got two apartments!'

And so Peter and I came to live within a block of each
other. Then Ray Ellington, the marvellous Goon Show
singer, moved in. Then, some time later, Spike turned up at
the same place. I think we were all there for about two years.
Then, almost in unison, we moved out. It may have had
something to do with a neighbourhood petition. Whatever
the reason, we scattered: Peter to a mini-mansion, Ray
Ellington to something elegant, Spike to a place close to
some other chums, and me to a ground-floor apartment. A
place with some solitude, so that Peter could come over and
we could bash the drums.

When I began to write about my life and times. I found myself
remembering things I had almost forgotten, and then trying
to interpret them. In the process, it has surprised me to learn
just how often things I thought were unconnected in my life,
suddenly met and connected. Such is the case in this story.

The only time I nearly missed being in London for a Goon
Show was in 1953. At the time I was driving a new Ford
Zephyr, which by English standards of those days was
considered a large car. Michael had been the first to buy a
Zephyr, and Peter was on the verge of getting one. Michael
had made a comment to his old pal, Stirling Moss, the racing
car driver, that the rear end of the Zephyr was a bit light,
and that it tended to swing a little on corners. Stirling Moss
suggested that we put weights in the boot. Of course
Michael's idea of a weight for the boot didn't turn out to be
a few bags of sand. He insisted that headstones would not

only do the job, but would provide a protective talisman. So we got them. (When I think of it now, I can't believe I went along with it.)

One weekend I travelled alone to a Saturday night appearance at a theatre about sixty miles from London. The next morning I got up early for the drive back, because we always recorded the Goon Show early on Sunday afternoon. I was only about two miles down the road when suddenly a Morris Minor came hurtling out of a side road, and I found myself swerving off the road into a field. Unfortunately, the ground was soggy, and the tyres sank into the mud. The Zephyr bucked like a mule and ended up cart-wheeling over on to its roof. The car was a wreck.

I suppose when I crawled out I should have come out a piece at a time, but when I looked for injuries the only things I could find were a slightly injured leg, a very sore buttock, several horrendous bruises and a very swollen lip. I mean a very, very swollen lip.

The next thing that happened is a coincidence I find hard to explain. As I was crawling out of the wreck, the very first person on the scene was the well-known singer, Fred Ferrari, from the Charlie Chester Show. He had been playing a date in a different town nearby, and here he was on his way back to London. So he hopped, and I limped, into his car, and we managed to arrive just in time for me to record the Goon Show. But I did have to play the harmonica — quite literally — side-saddle and side-mouthed.

Michael, of course, insisted that it was the talisman in the boot which saved me!

After a few days the lip was fine and so was my rear end, but what I didn't know was that a year later that leg injury would come back to bother me.

A few months after that Spike and Peter came to visit me to show me Peter's new car — a Volkswagen. There were not very many of these 'Beetles' in England in the early 1950s, and Peter seemed to take great pride in the eccentric looks of the little thing. But a short while later he, too, was involved in an accident, and the car was a mess. However, Peter himself didn't have a scratch, because it turned out that the VW had sort of surrendered, and bounced away from the crunch.

The next time I saw Peter I was surprised because he didn't have another Volkswagen. It was a big Ford Zephyr, with a great big weight in the boot. I asked him why he had changed cars and he said, 'I needed somewhere to carry my stone!'

It is the only answer I ever got.

But this shaggy dog story doesn't quite end there. The minor leg injury from my accident came back to bother me in 1954. By this time I had moved again, from a flat into the lower half of a house.

I had been having troublesome leg pain, so I went to see a doctor. Three specialists later I was told that I had to have a fairly minor operation on a vein in the leg. It took all three specialists to impress on me how 'minor' this was going to be. I didn't bother telling my friends about it because it was so 'minor'. Just one of those 'in a bit and out' hospital stays. But the specialists did suggest I have someone come in and, as they say, 'do' for me while I was recovering. They said that, perhaps, there might be some 'minor' pain.

Somehow, several of the London newspapers got wind of the operation and put out a story that Max Geldray was in hospital. One of the papers made reference to the leg injury being the result of a car accident. However, it did not mention that the accident was an old one.

The next thing I knew, I was back at home and fruit and bouquets of flowers were arriving from my friends, including Harry Secombe. Now the thing you have to understand about Harry is that, in addition to having the most loving and generous heart in the world, Harry does everything on the scale of the Pyramids. His basket of fruit and flowers half filled the room. I remember the bouquet was made in the shape of a horseshoe — similar to the kind put round the neck of a winning racehorse. The card said something like 'Have you up and racing around in no time'.

About an hour after that Peter telephoned. He was very upset. He insisted that he had to come right over.

For half an hour or so, I had to assure him I was all right. For the next half-hour I had to explain to Peter, who was

very hurt, why I had not told him about the operation.
Finally he relaxed and looked round the room at all my
flowers. He pointed at the biggest bundle in the corner.
'Where did that come from?'

When I told him it was from Harry his teeth, his jaw and
his hands clenched. His face grew red and he shook his head.
He looked about as forlorn and distressed as I have ever seen
him: as though he had done something unforgivable.

'Why don't I do things like that?' he lamented. 'Why
don't I think of things like that?'

It was such a strange over-reaction, so much too
self-critical, that I didn't know how to respond. Finally I
said, 'It doesn't matter . I'm OK, Pete. And anyway, you
are here.'

But for about two minutes he didn't say anything. And
then suddenly his face brightened, and he spoke in a tone
that sounded as though he had totally forgotten what had
just happened.

'I have a new car, Ploogie. A Rover,' he told me. 'I'm
going to take you for a ride.'

I told him that my leg was too sore and that, anyway, I
couldn't walk. He was always strong so he picked me up
gently in his arms, carried me out through the front door,
and sat me down on the luxurious leather front seat of his
fantastic Rover. The leg hurt, but that new Rover almost
made it all worthwhile.

We drove for quite a few minutes and Peter was very
animated. Finally he stopped near a busy cross street,
hopped out and said, 'You wait here.'

I told him I would try — although I might be a bit tempted
to crawl somewhere.

Peter was gone for about twenty minutes and when he
came back there were two men trailing behind him. They
were carrying three large boxes. After the parcels were
loaded in the boot, he pointed his thumb to the back, like a
hitch-hiker, and said, 'For you.'

When we got home and opened the boxes it turned out to
be a hi-fi set. Each and every one of the parts was wrapped
up like a birthday present. He and I spent most of the day

putting it together and playing with the sound.

I think my leg recovered in half the time because of that.

After I left England, Peter went on to a career that was astonishing. Although we were many miles apart, and no longer met that often, we never lost touch with each other. And he was always an exceptional friend. Once, when he was in Los Angeles, he telephoned and I casually asked about his ex-wife Ann. I said I would like to see her again. He said, 'Would you really, Ploog?' In a minute or so he hung up.

About an hour later he called me and said, 'She'll be here from London the day after tomorrow!' At first I couldn't follow who he was talking about, and then he mentioned that he had booked Ann and her husband in to the Bel Air Hotel. Later she was to tell me that when he phoned and said arrangements had been made for her, and her husband too if he wanted to go, she couldn't believe it. She said to me, 'Max, he made it sound as though he had to do this for you!'

And, for whatever reason, I believe he felt he had to.

The last communication I ever had from Peter was a letter from Switzerland, written on Christmas Eve a few months before his death. I have censored a couple of personal references that are in it, but the rest of it I would like to share with you.

25th December 1979

My dear Max,

Please try to excuse me for not writing to you before now. I have been in Paris making a film, 'The Fiendish Plot of Dr Fu Manchu', the film in which I thought I could find a part for you, but alas you look too Jewish!

The result should be very funny. Half Goon with a touch of Monty Python. My new film just opened in LA and NY *you should see*. Its called 'Being There' and I'm proud to say I'm playing a feature role almost completely straight for a nice change. Please do see it Max as its been my ambition for six years to get hold of the book. Hal Ashley the director and I made a tryst that neither of us would make it without the other. I look quite plump in it which was *deliberate*, I wanted the character to look stocky. However now I have lost almost 30lbs!, and have made myself rather weak in the process, but it was necessary for Fu Manchu, or me maybe. I have the photographs you sent me and I will keep them if you don't mind for reference.

The enclosed cutting of you with the Duke, Spike sent to me. I agree with what he says in his letter!!

I'm just going to open the Christmas presents now so I'll sign off and try my best to write more often.

Lots of love to you both and a prosperous 1980.

Ploogie — Pete

10

Changes

THE LAST GOON Show in the tenth series was broadcast on
28 January 1960. That was it: the end of the Goon years. I
suppose at some time or other in my life I've used that old
cliché 'A change is as good as a rest', but if someone had
said that to me just then I would have said it was bunk. Quite
a few other things in my life seemed to be changing — and
ending — at the same time. Things that, apparently, had
simply run their course! Changes which left me feeling lost
and constantly unsettled. But I have to go back further in
time — back to the war, in fact — to tell you about the other
things which converged on me at the end of the Goon years.

I have sometimes felt cheated when I have read a book
about someone's life, and found the writer implying more
than he told. I confess, I am about to do that myself right
now. This is a part of my life I have locked away in an
emotional cupboard. Even just opening the door ajar brings
back things I would prefer to keep locked away.

In 1942 I had met a young girl. She was a pretty Scottish
lass. But then quite a few women in my life were pretty. She
was a singer and we shared a love of music. But then lots of
females love music. What made her special to me was that
she was someone with a sympathetic ear. Someone who
seemed to be always there when I came to London on leave
from the Army. At that time my life was full of insecurity
and change. I was going off to war. I lived in a strange land
with no family.Those were not exceptional circumstances,
there were thousands and thousands of people in the same
situation, but it produced different emotions in all of us. In
me it wrought a feeling of incompleteness. I began to think

the simple-minded thought that my life only needed a little fixing, like a puzzle with a piece missing. I thought, 'If only I could have someone just for me — someone to be here.' And I married Zaza.

This was probably unfair to her, for my true emotional distraction and salvation was my music, and I threw myself into it whenever I could. In the Army it was with James Kirk and Kees van Dyk and our group. After the war it meant making radio appearances and going on tour every time I had a chance. I don't think I was ready for married life, and I felt a great sense of indifference to it. Music seemed to be a protective screen, for me, and eventually that screen became the Goon Show and my Goon Show friends. But we were creatures of our time: because divorce was a sign of failure, Zaza and I stayed together for ten years. I don't like, as you can see, airing dirty linen in public.

By the early 1950s my marriage to Zaza had long since burned itself out. I don't know whose fault it was, or that it really matters now. I do know I felt relieved and depressed at the same time. Zaza probably felt the same way. I also know that I didn't quite like the feeling of being single — or perhaps it was being alone.

When someone asked me, 'Are you happy about this divorce, Max?' I found myself saying yes, and believing it. But there was a tightness in my chest, and I couldn't help wearing one of those dreary sad faces that all but your best friends avoid.

I was living alone in a small flat, although I didn't spend much time in the place: I always seemed to be busy playing at a theatre out of town somewhere. But when I was at home, the flat was always full of people — It seemed to have become a gathering place. Some of the people I would know, but most of them I didn't. And I found myself in that awful state of not wanting to be alone, but desperate to have some kind of privacy. I was looking for some stability and galloping away from any obligation. I told myself I really needed someone who would fall between the two extremes of taking over my life and merely passing through it.

I have always been very conservative, and very slow to

catch on to trends and life-styles, but when I decided to find that 'someone' I was anything but conservative. She was a ballet dancer. She was very talented, slim and graceful — and she had a face which turned heads. She was also eighteen years old. I was about to turn forty! She was someone I could look after: the first gift I gave her was a pair of boots because her feet were always cold.

I suppose that at first she was attracted to me because I was an older man, and something of a celebrity. I moved in show-business social circles that she found exciting. But Barbara wasn't looking for a way to sleep her way to stardom, though she wasn't an innocent vestal virgin either. She once told me that she stayed with me because I was her strength.

Much later in my life, when there was a teen-aged daughter in my family, as a father I would have been incensed at any forty-year-old man who pushed into my daughter's life. The motives of men who do that are suspect: 'There he goes, showing the world he's still the man about town!' Or, as they say in the States, 'He's letting us know he can still cut it.' Well, I think I made those same observations! I was shocked at myself. It is always easier to condemn the actions of someone else, and then make excuses for your own: 'I was different!' But I have come to believe, after all these years, that my coming together with Barbara had much less to do with masculinity, and much more to do with family! I wanted to do for her the things I should have done for Xaviere, if she had lived. I had missed nearly all the pleasure, and the responsibility, of having a sister. Mine was just a memory.

At first I found her spirit and her freshness contagious — just being with her made me feel comfortable and more alive, as though new hours and new days really did hold something special in store. But then it grew into something more: I found her smart and entertaining and witty. And surprisingly, for one so young, I found her to be caring.

I'm in my seventies now and it is a long way to look back for feelings, but it seems to me that for a very long time 'the bloom stayed on the rose'. We were together for one year, then it grew into two and three and five.

But when the bloom did come off, and when our relationship began to disintegrate, it was much more complex than a loss of freshness or her youth.

As time passed, Barbara became upset by the fact that her career was not moving along. I think she sometimes blamed me for taking so much of her time and attention. A dancer must dance, but there were no jobs, and Barbara could only continue her dance classes and pretend they were real. She turned to acting, taking some serious training at a Stanislavski school in London. Peter Sellers got her a couple of small parts in feature films he was making, but her career never did take off.

It was as though I was all she had left to cling to. As for me, for a while I behaved in the same way toward her, but with that significant difference.

'Max, you treat me like a young sister!' she told me. And I did: as though she was someone whose welfare and conduct and future I had to guard. At first she found it endearing, then it began to bother her. She was a woman in her twenties, and found my attitude patronizing. But somehow I wouldn't let Barbara grow up.

We began to argue more and more. And, over time, the arguments became caustic. I accused her of being immature. I told her she would never have a career if she didn't have discipline. She accused me of being an old fuddy-duddy. She said, 'You're not my guardian!' They seemed like gentle verbal hits, but they were the ones that hit right at the heart.

Barbara grew very depressed. She began to talk about herself in the past tense: 'I used to be a dancer . . .' 'I did act for a while . . .'

We stayed together for almost six years. Finally, I told her that if she was ever going to sort herself out we would have to spend some time apart. We needed some time, I said, to cool off and think things over.

I thought we would be apart for a very short time. Barbara very quickly agreed. She said she had been thinking about it herself, and we should try it for a while. So there was no great fighting, no scenes, no long teary confrontations. And we certainly didn't banish each other from our lives. We just parted in great sadness. Parted as it turned out, for ever.

After she left I became compulsive about work. I would go out on a booking any time, any place. But the anchor of my life, the Goon Show, was receding into history. The other anchor of my life, Barbara, married, but some time later committed suicide. To this day I find it all hard to believe. And that question 'Why?' is unanswerable. I harboured a great deal of guilt for a long time after that.

I don't know whether or not television was the culprit, but at the beginning of the 1960s variety shows in England were beginning to lose their popularity. Although I had a great deal of work at the time, touring the theatre circuit was dispiriting. Professional pride seemed to have taken a nose-dive. I found myself working in theatres where the greatest virtue of the pit band was the fact that it showed up. I would stand on the stage, blowing my brains out, and the band seemed to be fighting off the sandman.

And there was yet another reason I was feeling low. For the first time in my life my health seemed to be deteriorating too. I felt sickly and burned out! It wasn't that I was really ill, but I was unwell. I had never been unwell! My friends had always described me as a guy who didn't know how to catch a cold — someone who could eat an inner tube and never get indigestion.

Somewhere, inside, my body was telling me that it was time to move on. And so I decided to add change to my life, on top of change! I have no idea where this compulsion came from — to leave England, to leave a place where I was well established, and to leave all my friends — but it was there and it was strong.

It was a cold and rainy December in England, and so I decided the first thing I should do was get myself back into shape with a long vacation. Vacations were things I hadn't bothered with for twenty years. But old habits die hard, and within two days of making that decision, out of the blue, I had a call about a job in Australia.

The Australian Broadcasting Company was putting

together a large television special, and they wanted me to appear. The only question I asked was, 'What's the weather like?' When they answered 'Summer!' I was on my way.

I flew to Sydney via Karachi and Singapore: thirty-six hours of travel. Thirty-six hours of engine sounds; of landings and take-offs; of ears plugging and popping; of meals from a tray; of sleeping in my clothes in a space the size of a pup tent; and weather that shook us around as though the plane was dissolving. By the time we landed I felt it was as though I was listening to the world through a beer barrel. But I did the show, I lay on the beach, I played in several night-clubs and recorded a short radio series, and lay on the beach. Four weeks had stretched into eight, but I began to feel like myself again.

When it was time to go back, I thought to myself, 'There must be a better way of getting back to England than the mobile death-wish I took coming out! I discovered that I could travel back to England with stop-overs. I went via Hawaii, to San Francisco and Los Angeles. Instead of thirty-six hours it took me twenty days to get back. But the stay in Los Angeles was to change everything.

In Los Angeles I looked up my old pal Johnny Fresco, and a few other musicians I had known in Europe. Johnny was working for the American Broadcasting Company, several of the others played with studio bands, but a lot of them had other jobs, in real estate or other businesses. There wasn't any sense of failure in that, because they all said more or less the same thing: 'This is the way we make survival money. We still get to play. But we want no part of being on tour again!' It was good to hear that other people felt the way I did, and I thought, 'Could it be the answer to move here?'

But once again, as I was thinking about permanent change, something came up. I was only back in England a matter of a week when I had another job offer. This time at sea!

The job was aboard the *Queen Elizabeth*, and I was to be part of the entertainment package offered passengers leaving Southampton for New York. There were two distinct varieties of travellers on the *Queen Elizabeth* in those days. The first group was made up of those who were going somewhere. Preferring sea travel, and having the time, they were on their way to do business, to meet people or to spend some time on the other continent. They were a very decorous group, made up mostly of upper-crusters or emigrants. The second group was simply on a voyage, and the ship was their way of leaving themselves behind. They ate, drank, danced, partied and philandered as though they were Olympic events.

I found myself falling in with the party-goers. When we docked I would get off the boat denouncing obesity, swearing off Bacchus and promising priestly vows for ever. Or at least until the next sailing!

Over the next six months I travelled on four of those four-and-a-half-day ocean crossings — back and forth from Southampton to New York. Then I thought to myself, if I don't get out of this, my life is going to have all the permanency of a passenger list. So I swore off the sea for ever, packed my bags, and took a one-way trip by plane. This time all my worldly possessions were in five suitcases!

It would be logical to think that I went to Los Angeles and Hollywood because of show business. But the truth is that it was because of friends, and their ideas about what a new life in Los Angeles could be like for me. But I wasn't there a month before I was back in an old groove.

I ended up taking a booking to appear in Reno, Nevada.

If you have never been to Reno I can tell you that it is a place which bills itself as 'The Biggest Little Town in the West'. The 'biggest' comes from the fact that it is full of big-time gambling, big-time show business and big-time glitz. But there is nothing else big about it. It is not big in heart, nor big in spirit. You have the feeling that you are living in a place where superficiality and being transient are the norms, where a fifteen-minute conversation at a bus stop is an enduring relationship and kids only get a six-year option on their parents.

Mind you, I did have marvellous opportunities there — I

worked with Dinah Shore, Billy Daniels, Sarah Vaughan and several other top-liners. And, as a result, I had the chance to appear on the Steve Allen Show out of New York, and the Dinah Shore Show out of Hollywood. I should have been ecstatic. But I only felt unsettled and uneasy!

I had the feeling that I was going to remain a stranger for ever if I didn't settle down somewhere in America. Obviously, Reno wasn't the place, so I went back to L.A., got myself a job playing harmonica in a local bar, and set about planting some roots. Luckily I met a girl named Susan.

Susan was a small, gentle, pretty and very vulnerable girl, who loved to laugh. And it was hard to understand where the good spirits came from, for Susan — a divorcee with three children — had had a very troubled time.

With my track record for commitment and permanency, who would have thought that I would opt for, along with the woman I loved, the parenthood of an eight, ten and thirteen-year-old? But it was only a matter of weeks before I proposed to Susan, and soon the five of us found ourselves moving into a small bungalow in the San Fernando Valley. I got myself a steady daytime job not far from my house — as a department store clothing salesman! I had planted enough roots to start my own forest!

Roots are a fine thing, and the first years of our marriage remain among the happiest of my lifetime. In the second year we had a son, Philip, a robust little bundle that the other kids adored, and a pure gift from heaven for Susan and I. Pardon me for being sentimental, but I have marvellous kids! But after about seven years there was one thing in my life that was causing regret: to all intents and purposes, I had become an ex-harmonica player and I hadn't replaced the music of my life with anything I could get my teeth into. I did want to do something involving, something that would give me the feeling that I was doing something more than merely making a living. And so, that summer of 1970, I pricked up my ears and listened intently when, during a very casual conversation, a friend mentioned to me that my church, Christian Science, had a job opening in Boston,

Massachusetts. The job was at the *Christian Science Monitor*, as a regional sales supervisor in the circulation department.(The *Monitor* is one of the most outstanding national newspapers in this or any other country.)

Why, you may ask, did I, a non-newspaper person, want to gallop off to join the fifth estate? And why, you may further ask, all the way across the continent? Let us not talk logic here. Let us talk change!

For any of you unfamiliar with Massachusetts, it is a state in the north-eastern part of the United States. It covers about 8,258 square miles and the capital is Boston. If any of you English readers think 'Massachusetts' is a funny name, I must tell you that the place was named through a company charter, drawn up in England in 1629. The Massachusetts Bay Company then established a colony on Massachusetts Bay. By 1630 the colony was called Boston. So you see, the English are not allowed to make fun of the name! But don't ever try to say it with your teeth out!

I really enjoyed working at the *Monitor* and (as that piece of information about Massachusetts shows) I learned a great deal while I was working there. Unfortunately, I sometimes felt as though I was back on tour, because I found myself travelling for the *Monitor* all over the States and through large areas of Canada. I found out I had come to hate making a living by travelling!

Another thing I found out was why they put the sound 'achu' right in the middle of the name Massachusetts. Boston was so cold that in winter everyone who went outside was constantly looking behind, checking to see what had broken off! Swinging your arms could be fatal!

Susan and I and the kids, who were now young adults, decided that at the end of that year, 1972, we would go back to Los Angeles. I would even go back to the clothing business — as long as I could live in a place where I could stop looking behind me all the time for my lost parts! We were in the midst of planning our move back to Los Angeles when a letter from England arrived. And — surprise, surprise — we ended up taking a short trip to England first!

11

The Last Goon Show of All

BY 1972 I had been in the United States for eleven years, married to Susan for ten, and the last Goon programme had been recorded a dozen years earlier.

During all these years I had kept in contact with Harry, Spike and Peter — there were letters and postcards and the occasional telephone call. And I often saw Peter when he was in Hollywood. But it is understandable that as the years go by, and you see little of each other, you begin to have less and less in common with your friends.

I suppose that is why people who go to reunions find themselves skipping quickly over the 'How are you?'s and the 'What are you doing?'s, and pulling out shovels to dig up nostalgia as soon as they can. But somehow the Goons never lost sight of each other. Although the mail was infrequent, no matter who wrote the letter it was always full of current news about the others, as though we had all been together just a few months ago.

Over the years there had been talk about the possibility of having a Goon Show reunion on the BBC, but I don't think any of us ever thought it would really happen. And in fact it never *would* have happened if it hadn't been for a very, very special occasion.

In 1972 the Beeb, or Beep Beep Cee (as the Goons affectionately called it), was about to celebrate the fiftieth anniversary of BBC Radio. The BBC had a fairly impressive plan for the celebration. There was to be a long look back at their broadcast history, broadcasting the earliest recordings, playing from the archives the programmes and the people who were keys to the BBC's role in wartime, peacetime, the arts, the sciences, and in English life generally. They were also going to do 'specials' as a form of birthday salute. One such 'special' was to be a Goon Show.

The letter I had received came from John Browell, who had produced the Goon Show for quite a few episodes in the last years of production. John said that they were going to reassemble everyone at the Camden Theatre in London, on Sunday 30 April 1972. He said, it seems everyone will be there! He said, come!

I gave the possibility careful and considered thought for several nanoseconds, then I found myself jumping up and down. I knew that being back with Peter, Harry and Spike would make me feel full of energy — anxious to run and talk, to be in their company and laugh, to sit quietly and feel the peace and joy of people I had known for so long. It seems I had decided to go!

With Susan and little Philip in tow, I arrived in London the day before the production.

We had hardly settled into our room at the hotel, when the phone rang. It was John Browell, and he was pleased to know I was there, because I was the last out-of-towner on his list. Then he said something which really surprised me, 'It's too bad about Wally Stott!'

When I asked 'What about Wally?' he said, 'Oh, didn't you know? Wally has declined to be on the show!'

Wally had been the musical arranger on the Goons from our very first broadcast. Then, after the completion of the second series, in July of 1952, he had taken over from Stanley Black as conductor of the orchestra. Wally had always been very important to that programme — and especially to me. He had written every arrangement I had ever played on the Goon Show. And we had worked on many other projects together, including making records.

Wally wasn't just someone I'd worked with, he was a great influence — someone who was very much my musical mentor. I was dumbfounded to find out that he had turned down a Goon Show! Knowing Wally as I did, I'd have said that he was the kind of person who would have swum in from the Falklands to be there.

When I asked other people about it, I got a second surprise. Not only did no one know why he had refused, no one had seen him! Wally Stott had been one of the busiest and most successful arranger/conductors in England, and he hadn't been seen for a year and a half. I was certain there was something desperately wrong, and that Wally had a major illness — an illness which was probably terminal.

I hadn't been in touch with Wally for about two years, but I knew some of his old friends and I telephoned round. No one seemed to know what was wrong, or where Wally was. I made about eight or nine calls before I was finally able to locate someone who had a telephone number.

Wally's second wife answered the phone. At first her manner was very stiff, and she seemed very remote. But when I convinced her that I really was Max Geldray, all the way from Los Angeles, she began to thaw, and I had the feeling she was not going to hang up on me.

She told me that she and Wally had moved from London about two years ago, and were now living on its outskirts. And while she made it obvious that she was very happy to hear from me, there was still some strain and reservation in her voice. And there was also something mysterious about the whole thing. When I asked to speak to Wally, she would only say, 'No, Max, let me drive over and get you.'

She would say no more.

The story I am going to tell you was totally unexpected. I tell it because it is an extraordinary story of two people's love and devotion to each other. It is a love and devotion which has gone far beyond the barriers of what most of us have faced in our lives.

Wally had been married a number of years and had children. However, although I had never had any sense of it, Wally had had a life-long mental struggle with gender identity. A fact that, for all those years, he had kept sealed tightly inside himself.

It is difficult to explain what 'gender identity' means, but it has very little to do with sex, and it is very seldom related to homosexuality. It has to do with the way you live your life — with the sex gender you are inside.

Wally's children grew up, his first wife died — and then he met his second wife. To quote Wally, 'It was only because of her love and support that I then was able to deal with the trauma, and begin to think about crossing over that terrifying gender border.'

It was decided that Wally would fly to a private clinic outside England. There he would have treatment to begin to deal with his problem. Wally would have a sex-change operation. Wally, in fact, was now female. Complete with a female name.

To be sure, I was shocked. This was something totally unexpected in someone I had known for twenty-five years. But it didn't take me very long to find out that, in all the ways that mattered, the person I found now was still the person I had known. And I was so relieved to find out that Wally wasn't dying, it didn't seem all that serious. It seemed like an anti-climax!

Have you ever had this experience? Someone tells you about something hilarious which happened to them — they stand there laughing and can hardly get it out, while you stand there with a plastered grin trying desperately to find a way to react, and then it falls flat? I think that's where the expression, 'Well, I guess you had to be there!' comes from. As for the reunion of the Goons on The Last Goon Show of All, I will say, right away 'You had to be there .'

That Sunday in April of 1972 was certainly an entertaining, fulfilling and sentimental experience for me. But it was also something else. If you have ever been at a reunion of veterans who fought together, you will have some idea of a feeling which the Goons shared. Of course our reunion wasn't about battles, it was filled with memories of laughs and songs and good times together. But there was some parallel in our feelings. When you put a group who fought together in the same place, they give off an inner feeling of camaraderie, and of a very special time in their lives. Emotions which can never really be shared with anyone outside. And Spike, Peter, Harry and I, no matter where we were now, or what we had done since, had shared those years with that same kind of very special flavour.

Perhaps the studio audience did sense that somehow, for we were greeted like conquering heroes, and we could feel the love and the joy bouncing up in their cheers.

Wally Stott wasn't at that Goon Show, and I think that is very understandable. But the two of them weren't only keeping themselves cloistered from the public, they were keeping themselves apart from everyone else as well — from family and friends, and the musical community. They had shielded themselves in this way for almost a year and a half, unsure about how the world would now accept them. And then they decided it was time to come out of their cocoon, and they did it in a brilliant way.

They threw a huge party, inviting every relative, friend and colleague they could remember. Almost all of them came. For a long while the atmosphere was strained: people seemed to be standing around in small circles, curious, embarrassed and very uncertain. Then, one of their friends, an Aunty Mame type, who wore large flowered hats and garden party dresses, shouted out, 'Oh, for goodness' sake, let's get on with the party!' And the awful pressure seemed to lessen, and everyone could feel the embarrassment and discomfort, or whatever it was, begin to melt away.

By the time the English tabloids got hold of the story, and plastered it all over England, the two of them were not hiding their faces from anyone.

Today, they live in the Los Angeles area, and I see them fairly often. To see them together is to see two people who have grace and intelligence, and a great tenderness toward each other. Music is still a great creative force in their lives. In fact, it is most probably more creative than ever before. Emmy Awards, for the scoring of television specials, sit on the grand piano. There have been half a dozen other nominations for Emmys, and several for Academy Awards too. And hanging on the walls is a gallery of autographed pictures of musicians, directors, actors, composers, and even royalty. It is evident that a great many people are devoted to them.

If the events of their lives have been unusual, it is also fair to say that their lives have been creative, thoughtful and, in their togetherness, extremely rich.

12

The Final Phase

I CALL THIS the final phase because no matter how long I go on living, I really don't expect my life to alter much from what it is today. At least, I hope it won't. (Positive things, like winning the lottery, being excepted).

We hadn't been back from England very long before we moved from Boston back to the West Coast. It was 1979, and there I was back in Los Angeles working in men's clothing again. I had a strong feeling of *déjà vu*!

Over the years I had often visited Palm Springs, especially after my marriage to Susan. She had a number of relatives there, including her father. Around April 1973 he became quite ill, and, since he was also very elderly, Susan and I decided to move to Palm Springs to take care of him. Let me explain that I wasn't thinking about working there: I just wanted a few gigs to make a few bucks. I had a state of semi-retirement in mind. For a while that is exactly how it worked out!

I think it was Sigmund Freud who came up with the theory that nothing significant happens in your life without your having a large hand in it. He didn't mean that if you were walking down the street, and a building fell on you, that you had willed it to happen, but that most of the things in life that make us happy or unhappy are things that we have helped to happen. Whether that's consciously or unconsciously. I have always believed in that.

I've known a lot of people who had a flair for happiness, and I suppose just as many who went around walking into the wall of life, complaining hourly about how unlucky they were.

Then there are those who think they have bad luck, but celebrate the event like good little martyrs. You know the type — the ones who want to tell you about their operations! I bring this up because, when I had settled in, the martyrs and the complainers seemed to be invading my life.

There we were, the neighbours and I, sitting around in carefree semi-retirement in Palm Springs, California. The houses in the district were modest, but bright and comfortable. The place was full of people around our own age. And the sun always shone on the swimming pool a hundred yards from my house. Occasionally I would stir from the nest and take a job, playing at a banquet or a party or a wedding. Happy as a clam, right? Wrong! I found myself sitting around a pool, or in someone's kitchen, with a small group of neighbours who were living the same life-style as I was, but all the while complaining, or revelling in their unhappiness, or developing a whole set of medical symptoms and aches that scared the pants off me. They played golf. They had martinis. They ate. They slept. They played golf, they . . .

These people weren't living life, they were re-cycling it. I decided I'd better do something a little more than merely stir from the nest. I remembered Freud!

I got myself a job very quickly after that, playing at a place called the Trinidad Bar — not a very appropriate name for a bar that featured jazz! Then one night, as Susan and I were sitting between sets, a man came up to me and introduced himself as Doctor Hirshleifer. He said he was a jazz fan, and that he had founded the Stroke Center in Palm Springs. He asked me if I would like to volunteer to put on a show for the patients.

The very next week, I did. I told the patients a little about the history of the harmonica, played a few tunes and got a few gentle laughs. I decided I would go back the following week, too. But this time I changed things considerably. I brought along a dozen small mouth organs and asked my audience of patients what they thought about forming a group. And we did — and we all played. Well, sort of.

That was nine years ago. I have gone to the Center every

week since then. The strokers and I have formed a group called 'The Blow Hards'. And every week there are these people — of all ages and all types of background — trying their best to play along. I think they do it because they want to show themselves, and the world, that they really can still manage some things in life. I know all that sucking-in and blowing-out helps with their breathing. Even holding the mouth organ up to their lips gets the body moving. And it's good therapy, because we also laugh a lot, too.

I remember one patient, a young surgeon in his early thirties, who had hardly started his career in medicine. It isn't hard to understand why he was bitter and unresponsive. His parents used to come to see him, and he would glower at them and never say a word. Somehow one day I got him, very tentatively, going along with the group. He forgot himself for a few minutes. Suddenly he started to laugh. It may have been a black kind of humour — he was laughing at himself because he couldn't inhale — but he laughed. I thank God for that moment. It was lovely, and I will never forget it.

Seeing those people — the strokers — and being involved with them was something that changed my life even more than going back to work at the Trinidad Bar. I felt useful!

My next piece of volunteerism came about in a way I would never have wished for.

We had had a family tragedy some time before, in which our son, Timmy, died after a year of illness. The details aren't important, but of course the loss was. For a very long time after his death Susan stopped being herself. And with her father's illness her spirits got worse.

I didn't sense deep depression, but I could certainly feel her mood swings and periods of sudden grief. She was drinking more often. Not a great deal, we thought, just a couple when she got home after work, then another one or two at dinner. Perhaps another late in the evening. Occasionally I'd notice that she had gone to bed early and taken a drink with her. And if she was a little tipsy I never knew it. I had only seen her drunk once, and that had happened years before, after a large and long party. So I didn't think of her as a 'drinker'. I couldn't help noticing that the drinking was increasing and more regular, but why should I face up to Susan, or nag her, when she was in such emotional turmoil?

When I look back I can see that one of the most fortunate things to happen at that time was that Susan had an accident at the house. She slipped in the bath and, while she wasn't really hurt, she had a nasty gash on the side of her cheek. When we got her to the hospital the doctor gave her a very thorough examination and said that, apart from needing some stitches in the cheek, she would be all right. But then he surprised us by asking about her drinking problem. The blood tests, he said, showed that she had a very high level of alcohol. Of course Susan described her drinking as light and infrequent. It was just because of stress right now! But I think that was the first time that the family could really see that that was not the case, that she had been drinking much more than any of us had cared to notice or wanted to acknowledge. The doctor took a long history, and at the end of it suggested that my beautiful wife, this fine mother, was probably an alcoholic! A drunk!

As I've mentioned earlier, I now work at a centre for the treatment of people who have problems with alcohol and other drugs. This is the Betty Ford Center, and it's located in Rancho Mirage, California.

When treatment is given, it is not only the alcoholic patient who comes under care, it becomes a family affair. The premise is that the addiction so pervades the lives of all the people who surround the addict, that they are suffering from the disease too. I have seen this shown over and over again in family sessions at the Betty Ford Center — wives on the brink of collapse; children filled with resentment and scorn; parents full of a sense of failure. Whatever its form, they are people filled with hurt, and they are scarred. As you can understand, a great deal of treatment has to do with rebuilding lives and relationships. In effect, everyone has to recover.

I have never had an alcohol problem myself, but three members of my family did — with almost devastating results. As a family member I went through the BFC treatment. I was so affected by the experience that later on I started to do volunteer work at the Center, and eventually I joined the staff. It was the beginning of an education for me.

Among the first patients at the brand new Betty Ford Center was Susan Geldray. And that experience changed both our lives. The saying is that the treatment at the Ford Center helps you get in touch with your feelings. Susan and I did miraculously well in the programme — and, in a sense, re-found each other.

For the first time in a long time Susan and I began to know each other. To talk to each other. That is a strange description for a couple who had shared so much together for so many years. But for a long time we hadn't really looked at each other, or listened to each other. And I suspect that before this we had never been completely open with each other. We both had always had a problem with telling people how we felt. I suppose as I say that to you I am telling you that I learned a lot about myself!

The Center is not like a hospital, you see. Conversation — and understanding — are therapy.

Imagine getting to the point, for the first time in your life (when you are damned near sixty-five), where you can say you have come to know yourself! And even like yourself!

I volunteered at the BFC after that. I wanted to be a part of it any way I could. I started off picking up patients at the airport, answering phones, taking around mail and carting people off for medicals. It felt like very important work to me!

I have been working full time for five years in the counselling process. I feel that working at my age keeps me alive and vital, because I am working with some exceptional people, and doing something meaningful.

It seems that almost everyone has heard of the Betty Ford Center. I suppose in the field of alcohol and drug treatment Mrs Ford has become something of a living icon. Well, she is special — a lovely woman who works very, very hard for the Center and its causes.

People are apt to think of this place she founded as a spa for the rich, or a retreat for movie stars and other kinds of celebrities. But the BFC is anything but a spa. And it is hard to believe that it is one of the least expensive treatment centers in all of the United States. But that is not important — it is the success and the good that it does that matter. I may be at the age where I creak a little, but I sure am happy to be there.

It is now 1989. And except for dear Peter Sellers the Goons are still around. Spike Milligan is a best-selling author these days, and is as passionate and volatile as ever, still displaying those brilliant sparks of wit, charm and fun for which he is famous.

Michael Bentine, one of our originals, is someone I see often in the winter, here in Palm Springs. He still has great vibrancy and humour. With his marvellous memory he often sits and holds me enthralled with memories of times and places and people I seem long since to have forgotten.

Harry — now 'Sir' Harry — Secombe is blessedly unchanged. He works continuously, and still is the same human being with enough warmth to change the climate of Europe.

Susan and I lead very active lives. And while our youngest, Phil, is twenty-four, we have grandchildren to start the cycle all over again.

I do admit though — just occasionally, mind you — that I find my memory creeping back in time. And for those few moments I yearn for something else.

My lips seem to take over, and all by themselves they take a shape.

Then my hands cup, and in my imagination they come up to my lips.

They hold an invisible instrument.

The music begins.

And, once again, I'm the Goon with the wind.